Listen
to the
Squawking
Chicken

AMY EINHORN BOOKS
Published by G. P. Putnam's Sons
a member of Penguin Group (USA)
New York

Listen to the Squawking Chicken

When Mother Knows Best,
What's a Daughter to Do?

⊃G

Elaine Lui

AMY EINHORN BOOKS
Published by G. P. Putnam's Sons
Publishers Since 1838
Published by the Penguin Group
Penguin Group (USA) LLC
375 Hudson Street
New York, New York 10014

USA • Canada • UK • Ireland • Australia
New Zealand • India • South Africa • China

penguin.com
A Penguin Random House Company

Library of Congress Cataloging-in-Publication Data

Lui, Elaine.
Listen to the Squawking Chicken : when mother knows best,
what's a daughter to do? : A memoir (sort of) / Elaine Lui.
p.   cm.
ISBN 978-0-399-16679-2
1. Lui, Elaine.   2. Mothers and daughters—United States.
3. Chinese Americans—Biography.   4. United States—Biography.   I. Title.
CT275.L488A3   2014   2014002064
306.874'3092—dc23
[B]

Printed in the United States of America
3   5   7   9   10   8   6   4   2

Book design by Gretchen Achilles

For Dad and Jacek,
who get squawked at too . . .

Contents

Introduction *1*

1. Walk Like an Elephant, Squawk Like a Chicken *5*

2. Never Bring Home an Umbrella off the Street *19*

3. Where's My Money? *49*

4. You Will Be Thanking Me for Your Entire Life *71*

5. I Should Have Given Birth to a Piece of
Barbecue Pork *91*

6. Miss Hong Kong Is a Whore *119*

7. Don't Cut Bangs over Thirty *139*

8. Why Are You Dating a Triangle-Head? *177*

9. That's So Low Classy *207*

10. You Only Need One True Friend *233*

Epilogue *267*

Acknowledgments *271*

Listen
to the
Squawking
Chicken

You Look Like Dried Monkey Flakes

That's what my ma, the Chinese Squawking Chicken, tells me when she thinks I look like shit on television. Monkeys are skinny. A poorly moisturized monkey is not only skinny but brittle. No one wants to look like dried monkey flakes. Most people think I'm exaggerating at first when I talk about the Squawking Chicken. But once they actually do spend some time with her, they understand. They get it. Right away. She's Chinese, she squawks like a chicken, she is totally nuts, and I am totally dependent on her. If she says I look like dried monkey flakes, even if everyone else thinks I'm camera-ready, I believe that I look like dried monkey flakes.

This is how it's been for me my whole life: every thought has been shaped by the Squawking Chicken; every opinion I have is informed by the Squawking Chicken; everything I do is in consultation with the Squawking Chicken. I navigate my life according to the subliminal map she's purposefully programmed into my head so that I can't tell the difference anymore whether it's my own choice or her choice. And that was probably her objective all along.

The Squawking Chicken has engineered my entire life, completely intentionally. She has always known who I was meant to be; I am who she's always wanted me to be. And she has spent my entire life pushing me in that direction, taking credit for it along the way. If I am happy and successful, it's because she guided me there. If I am unhappy and unable to meet challenges, it's because I didn't listen. *Teng* means "to listen" or "to hear" in Chinese. The expression for "obedience" in Chinese combines *teng* with the word for "speak," which is *wah. Teng wah* literally means "listen to what I say." I have been listening to the Squawking Chicken for forty years.

Is it self-fulfilling prophecy that I did indeed fail, and sometimes disastrously, on the occasions when I disregarded her instruction? One night she told me, after I'd come home from college and finished all my exams, that I was too tired to go out to see my friends, that my friends would still be there tomorrow when I'd had a good night's sleep, and, most ominously, that I would regret not staying home. Half an hour later as I was backing the car out of the garage, I realized too late that I'd forgotten to close the rear door. It caught on to the wall while I was reversing and, as I hit the gas, the entire door came off. I didn't listen to the Squawking Chicken and the Squawking Chicken was right.

"You are controlled by your mother," a colleague told me recently. It was said with a mixture of fascination and pity, mostly pity. Indeed, some who have observed our interactions do shake their heads, feeling sorry for me that I've been held hostage, emotionally and mentally, by a mother living vicariously through her daughter. They're not wrong about the control, but they are definitely wrong about living vicariously. The Squawking Chicken has her own story, and I'm just a part of it.

I decided to write this book during Ma's recovery from a long and potentially fatal illness. At first, I wanted to give her something to look forward to, something to get better for. But in telling her story, I realized that I was actually doing it for me—which is what always happens when I think I'm doing something for her. It turns out I'm the one who's benefiting. In this case, it's to convince myself that even if the squawking stops, I will always be able to hear it.

CHAPTER 1

Walk Like an Elephant, Squawk Like a Chicken

If the world operated on mute, my ma would seem to you like any other Chinese lady—on the short side of average, small-boned, but obnoxiously dressed. Think rhinestones everywhere, and if not rhinestones then sequins, and if not sequins then feathers. Sometimes all of it at the same time. Her favorite outfit is a denim suit with rhinestone-encrusted patches on the back and up and down the legs. She purposefully wears it with the collar turned up. Like the irresistibly catchy hook in the worst song you've ever heard, she finishes her China Woman Elvis ensemble off with a pair of gold-and-silver Coach sneakers. If I'm really lucky that day, it'll be sunny out when we go for dim sum. And she'll keep her shades on as she walks into the restaurant, her entire head hidden underneath one of those massive sun visors regularly seen on Asians. People will wonder: Is it a movie star or a bag lady who's pillaged a donations bin in Vegas? The face that appears when she finally removes the sunglasses and the hat is so pretty it's almost ornamental. In other words, by appearance only, Ma seems harmless.

Turn up the volume and everything changes. As soon as you hear her, you'll never forget her. It's the voice, a voice that earned her the nickname Tsiahng Gai, Squawking Chicken, when she was growing up in Hong Kong. The volume is jarring, yes. You can't imagine that something so loud can come out so effortlessly and without warning. The Squawking Chicken doesn't give you time to acclimate to her decibel. It's one level, and it's all-out assault. But it's also the tone—sharp, edged and quick, not so much a booming roar that leaves silence after it lands, but a wailing siren that invades your mind, kind of like acid on the brain that results in permanent scarring.

Ma speaks to me mostly in Cantonese, the main Chinese dialect spoken in Hong Kong, with the occasional mangled English word thrown in for dramatic effect.

Here's an example. The following sentence is spoken entirely in Cantonese, with one exception. See if you can figure out what she means: "I don't like this sweater. The colley is so poor." What is "colley"? Hint: "colley" is not "collar." "Colley" is "quality."

Ma uses "colley" to describe not only inanimate objects

and clothing items but also people. Once we were shopping for vacuum cleaners and the salesperson was rude to her. "What colley does he have to talk to me like that?" Translation: "This man is not qualified to speak to me like that."

When she does have to speak in English, verb tense is a problem. It's a problem I have intentionally never corrected for her. I let Ma walk around telling people, "I am so exciting!"

What she means is that she is very excited. What comes out is so much more entertaining. Especially when you consider how loud she is.

Ma doesn't know how to have a discreet phone call, or a quiet conversation in the theater before the movie starts. Not only is she physically incapable of whispering, she also never wants to. Ma's philosophy is to talk loud and walk loud. Muhammad Ali floated like a butterfly and stung like a bee. Ma walks like an elephant and squawks like a chicken, and she has always taught me to do the same. It annoys her to see girls encouraged to behave otherwise.

She made this clear during a family gathering at my aunt's. It was dinnertime and we were all called to the table. My young cousin Lizzy was upstairs and we could hear her making her way down, thumping all the way to the kitchen. Her father shouted out, "Lizzy, don't walk so loudly! Walk like a lady!"

Ma didn't have much use for this particular uncle. She turned to me archly and remarked: "My grandfather always told me to walk like an elephant. It scares away the ghosts. Ah Leuy [my daughter], you should always walk like an elephant. A real woman doesn't creep into a room."

Traditionally, Chinese girls are raised to be cute and dainty. To smile demurely. To cover their mouths when they laugh, as if laughing is an activity too gregarious and inelegant to be considered proper form for a female. In Chinese culture, girls are often infantilized and objectified. They are told to leave the room when men are talking business. Their opinions are not solicited and when they are offered, it can become an embarrassment for their male partners. Girls are taught to not be *cho lo*, or rough. Their mannerisms should be delicate, their dispositions gentle. The language should never be offensive; "nice" Chinese girls never curse. As jarring as it is in Western society to hear swear words thrown around, it's even more offensive in Chinese culture. Foul language is used sparingly and usually restricted to men. And the Squawking Chicken. Ma has never observed the "boys only" gender restriction of swearing. She'll drop an F-bomb or even a C-bomb whenever she wants, and especially when she's in a scrap. There is no tiptoeing around where Ma is concerned, not with her feet and never with her mouth.

The Chinese Squawking Chicken has never crept anywhere. And she has never had a problem being heard. Unlike many Asian women of her generation who speak softly and behave demurely, my ma is always the first to offer her opinion, the first to speak up, even among those who believe that women are supposed to be soft and unassuming. Raised in a society that has traditionally encouraged subservient behavior for women, my ma was never the girl in the corner hiding her thoughts.

Over the years, some people have found her attitude, her voice and her demeanor repulsive, preferring women who congregate in small groups, too meek to go head-to-head with the men. But Ma has always been confident in any environment, from gambling in Hong Kong with gang members in her youth to teaching middle-aged Jewish housewives in Toronto how to play mah-jong. Her Squawking Chicken attitude has been the same no matter what: she believes she belongs anywhere. To me, she's always been the main event, dominating the spotlight no matter the setting, the ultimate scene-stealer.

Ma started in Yuen Long, a town on the western side of Hong Kong. Most of the action in Hong Kong happens in

Kowloon, situated in the southern area of the peninsula. When Ma was growing up, Kowloon was "downtown," the glamorous big city. Back then, Yuen Long was rural and unsophisticated and it took over an hour to get to Kowloon by bus and train. Apartment buildings were just being constructed. Most people lived in modest stone or wood houses clustered in villages fifteen minutes' walking distance from Yuen Long Main Road, a paved street that led to a few local pubs, restaurants and the open market. In those times, Yuen Long residents were considered hicks to the people who lived in Kowloon. The Squawking Chicken never thought of herself as a hick. Though she was born in Yuen Long, she always behaved as if she was from Kowloon. And, as it happens, Yuen Long started to develop into a more urban district just as she was coming of age, as though she willed it to grow up and be more cosmopolitan so that it could be worthy of her.

The Squawking Chicken was a classic big-city girl stomping around in a small pond, where girls were never taken seriously. In Yuen Long in the sixties and seventies, however, she was the only girl who had the balls to sit down for dominoes or mah-jong with the boys, beating them regularly and eventually earning their respect. She was so fierce that some of them ended up avoiding her, not wanting to tangle with a girl who could play as well as they could and then talk smack even louder than they would. Ma was assertive in a community that did not encourage assertiveness in women. Ma squawked for those who couldn't squawk for themselves. And so it was my young ma who volunteered to negotiate with the local triad (Chinese mafia) leaders when one of her friends fell behind on protection payments.

Back then, many people ran underground mah-jong dens out of their homes. To keep the police from interfering and shutting down the operations, each den paid a monthly "tax" in exchange for being left alone. The taxation system was managed by gangs. When Ma was in her late twenties and I was six years old and spending the summer with her in Yuen Long, the man who ran her favorite den was being threatened because he was two months' short, having had some family health problems. When she heard about the situation, Ma decided she had to go to the nightclub where the triad boss was known to hang out. I was in a fussy mood that day and I knew, even when I was little, that the only place worth being was where Ma was going; I refused to stay back and wait for her and I was complaining so loudly that I would have been a nuisance to the other mah-jong players if she left me behind.

It was wet and hot that afternoon, a typical Hong Kong summer day, and I remember Ma scolding me when I started whining about walking there in the heat instead of taking a taxi. "You could have stayed with the mah-jong aunties in front of the fan. But since you had to come, I'm not treating you like a princess." That was the only thing she said to me on our way there. After a few blocks, we turned right into an alley. There was nothing to it except for a glass door covered with a green neon sign.

I was thrilled to feel the blast of air-conditioning when we stepped inside. I couldn't see anything it was so dark. I held on tighter to Ma's hand as we made our way past a second door and into the club. She led me to the bar, told me to sit there quietly and wait for her, ordered me a drink with fruit cubes swirling at the bottom and told the server to give me extra cherries. I stabbed at the grape and pineapple bits in my glass with the cocktail umbrella and from my position across the lounge, I watched as she took a seat opposite an intimidating-looking man wearing a tank top with his leg hitched up on a table. She pulled a cigarette out of her purse. I could see the flame from a match in between her long red nails, and smoke drifting out of her mouth, framing her face. Then she started speaking.

I couldn't hear what she was saying from across the room, but I know she did most of the talking, pausing only to flick ashes into an ashtray now and again, the nail on her index finger tapping the end of the cigarette. Before long, the man was nodding and holding his hands up. Then suddenly we were back in the daylight, my eyes readjusting to the brightness, heading back to the mah-jong den, where Ma ceremoniously took her seat. "It's done. Let's play."

Ma was so gangster. But a gangster with nothing to hide, no secrets. Instead, her secrets, even though some of them were terrible, became her truths, because she was the first to squawk them out before anyone else, owning them before they could own her. In doing so, she taught me that if you can tell the story of the worst thing that has ever happened to you, you'll never be silenced.

The Squawking Chicken was born in 1950, the oldest of six children. Neither of her parents had steady jobs and they left her for the first few years in the family village to be raised by her grandmother while they worked sporadically. Ma's mother was in and out of restaurants, washing dishes or wrapping dumplings, and her father ran odds and ends for local gangsters, shaking down clients when they were behind on extortion payments. Any money earned was spent on the mah-jong table, which put them into debt most of the time, but occasionally lifted their circumstances. Ma was brought back to live with them during one particularly flush period when her parents returned home to the village to boast and show off. She didn't want to leave her grandmother with whom she was close and who she calls her "real" mother, the person who built her character. But it wouldn't look right, since her parents were now presumably well off, to live in the village and not be with her parents.

The highs of gambling never last long. And there was always a new dependent on the way. Ma looked after her siblings every day after school while her parents slept off their all-night mah-jong sessions. But she loved school and she remembers herself as a bright, engaged student even though her parents were never supportive of her studies. She only had time to study when the younger kids were finally in bed and after her parents had left for the gambling halls, reading by lamppost out on the street because she was forbidden to "waste" electricity. (This is totally the Chinese equivalent of the grandfather trope: I had to walk ten miles knee-deep in snow just to get to school.)

Soon, though, she had to quit. She'd just started Grade 10 and her parents noticed that she'd become rather attractive and could start earning money for the family waiting tables. So Ma was sent to work at a sketchy local night lounge. The regular patrons, mostly minor players in the local gangs, became fond of her sense of humor and sassy, no-shit attitude. They showed their affection by tipping her well and looking out for her when they could.

It was around this time that her mother took off with another man. Ma's father checked out and started disappearing for days on alcohol-fueled mah-jong benders. Ma had to care for her five brothers and sisters, relying on neighbors and sometimes even her gangster buddies. A few months later, her mother returned, having been abandoned by her lover, and now pregnant. Ma's parents reunited and they asked her to keep their secret. Ma helped her mother through her abortion, continuing to look after her siblings, managing the household as my grandmother recovered, making excuses and lying to neighbors and other family members who were curious about what was going on at home. Soon, my grandparents were carrying on like nothing had happened, thanks to the efforts of their dutiful eldest daughter. Ma was happy to have been useful to her parents. She complied with their requests without resentment and she thought that after this ordeal she would be more appreciated.

But soon after, on a night when her connections weren't around, Ma was raped on the way home from work. There was no sympathy from her parents when she stepped in the door, her clothes torn, her mouth bruised, her palms cut.

They did not offer to call the police. They did not help her clean herself up. Ashamed and despondent, Ma attempted suicide that night by swallowing pills. She remembers, through her haze, overhearing her parents discussing whether or not to help her and take her to the hospital. They ended up deciding not to, both to save money and also to save face, because Ma was the only one who knew all their secrets—her mother's affair and the aborted baby, her father's womanizing and drinking problem, their debts. With her gone, no one would ever find out. That was the night my ma started squawking. She forced herself to start vomiting and when she was finished vomiting she started screeching.

When Ma brought me back to Hong Kong years later, people used to tell me all the time about the night Ma started screaming. It's remembered like legend—that her screams rang through Yuen Long all night, that she screamed so hard and so violently it was like the gods were being summoned to deliver judgment upon her parents. Her screams were so incriminating, her parents actually skipped the gambling halls that night, hiding inside to avoid the neighbors, knowing that they'd been found guilty. Ma screamed to forget that she'd been violated; she screamed until the wound from her parents' treachery became a scar that permanently transformed her soul; she screamed to announce that she'd been reborn.

The next morning, she told her parents things were about to change. And they did. From that day on, all she had to do was look at them funny and they'd step back. That was when she started running her own life. She was fifteen.

Did you know that the phoenix is a breed of chicken that molts on a regular cycle? Ma was molting. She'd become the Chinese Squawking Chicken.

CHAPTER 2

Never Bring Home an Umbrella off the Street

⊃⒢

The Squawking Chicken never read to me at bedtime. This is partly because she's an immigrant. This is why I don't know *Goodnight Moon*. I read my first Dr. Seuss book in high school, when it was part of a class assignment on children's literature. But it wasn't just the language that prevented Ma from reading stories to me at night. Reading to children at night simply isn't part of traditional Chinese culture. Besides, Ma doesn't think there's much value in stories that encourage dreams and fantasy. She believes that children are perfectly capable of coming up with their own happy fantasies, and that "storytime" instead should be used to ready children for life's upcoming challenges.

I used to ask her all the time, "Why don't you ever tell me anything good, anything fun?"

And her answer all the time was, "Why do you need to

prepare for the good things that happen? They're good. They won't hurt you. Do you need advance notice for the arrival of happiness? Or would you rather have advance notice of the hard times? My job is to prepare you for the hard times. My job is to teach you how to avoid the hard times, whenever possible."

So instead of fairy tales, the Squawking Chicken told ghost stories, some of which she experienced herself. Many of my life lessons came from Ma's personal tales.

ഗ

Never Bring Home an Umbrella off the Street

When Ma was thirty, she was asleep alone one day in Hong Kong. The bed started shaking. She got up and checked if there was an earthquake. Nothing else seemed to be moving, nothing else was disturbed. She thought it was probably a bad dream and went back to bed. She'd just fallen back asleep when the bed started shaking again. It was rocking back and forth. Then she felt like she was being jumped on, hands all over her body, trying to push her off the bed. Except there was no one there.

Terrified, she scrambled out of the house and headed over to her favorite mah-jong den, hoping a few rounds would calm her down. It didn't help. She was still unsettled. She felt like she was surrounded by a dark cloud. She kept seeing shadows when there were no shadows. One of the other mah-jong players asked her what was bothering her. Ma explained what had happened in bed, feeling silly as she heard herself telling her friends that she'd been attacked by imaginary intruders. Almost everyone agreed that she was probably just stressed out or too tired, and encouraged her to keep playing. Except for one relative newcomer to the group sitting at another table. During a tea break, she came over to Ma and told her privately that it sounded like she had *jong gwai*. *Jong* is the word for "run into." *Gwai* means ghost. *Jong gwai* is a common expression in Chinese to describe someone who is acting strangely, out of the ordinary, like they've been possessed.

At this news, Ma cut out of the game and went to see a feng shui master. Feng shui masters are like spiritual advisors, well trained in feng shui principles, the ancient Chinese study of heavenly astronomy and earthly energy used to promote balance and well-being. A proper feng shui master is also familiar with the supernatural. He can give advice on where to best position a desk in the luckiest corner of a room to ensure maximum success and financial gain. He can also enter a space and detect the presence of positive and negative otherworldly forces. Many feng shui masters have capitalized on their talents and have turned their services into businesses. It's been a lucrative endeavor for a few of the top ones around the world. But for every legit feng shui master, there are five frauds. It's like good magic and black magic. A proper feng shui master uses his power to help people. An evil feng shui master exploits them.

Ma told the feng shui master what had happened in bed—how it felt like it was vibrating, and how, later on, she felt like she was being pushed and shoved by hands she couldn't see. The feng shui master asked Ma for her birth date, birthplace and exact time of birth. He studied her face, focusing on her eyes, closely examining her, silently, for several minutes. He took out some incense and let it burn, studying the pattern of the smoke. He made some notes on his scroll and used his abacus, flicking the beads back and forth, sometimes slowly, jotting down mystery calculations corresponding to Ma's birth information.

Finally he completed his assessment.

"You have very sharp eyes," he explained to Ma. "They help you see to your advantage, but sometimes they see too much. A dullness has descended on your face. It has come down from your eyes. You have seen something and what you have seen has blocked your vision. You must remove what is covering your eyes. You must remove the ghost. A ghost is what you have seen. And you will not truly see again until it leaves you alone."

The feng shui master sent Ma away with instructions to check her house for any recent additions. Had she picked up anything strange? Had something been moved? Had she inadvertently allowed a sinister presence to invade her space by creating a ghost-friendly environment?

Ma called her brother and asked him to go home with her because she didn't want to go back by herself. She thoroughly searched the apartment, looking for clues—anything that may have been rearranged or accidently shifted. She called the cleaning lady and asked her if she had changed anything the last time she was over. There was nothing out of the ordinary . . . until she remembered.

The week before, Ma had found an umbrella on the sidewalk on her way home. Thinking it would be useful, she brought it home and put it in the utility closet with the brooms and other cleaning products. Now Ma asked her brother to open the closet. She stood behind him, fearful. The umbrella was leaning up against the wall. And beside it were a boy and a girl, shivering and hungry, their hair matted against their gray, gaunt faces, black eyes filling with black tears, reaching out to her with rotting hands, pleading with her for help. Her brother snatched the umbrella and slammed the door. They ran out of the house, several blocks, to the local dumping ground. They lit the umbrella on fire.

Ma reported back to the feng shui master immediately. His eyes widened as soon as she said the word "umbrella." He stopped her right away. "Has no one ever told you that ghosts hide under umbrellas? Never pick up an umbrella off the street. An unwanted umbrella harbors ghosts that are waiting to claim a new home."

There was no more bed-shaking after that. And Ma never picked up an umbrella off the street again. Or anything else for that matter. Not money, not jewelry, *nothing*.

Ma told me this story one night when I was eight years old. I was pissed off at her because she hadn't let me keep a really pretty bracelet that I'd found lodged between the seats on the subway that day. She told me to shove it back into the crack where I'd found it and initially I refused. I still remember her red nails snatching the red band out of my hands, wedging it back into the cushions. My tantrum was immediate. I started wailing so loudly people moved away from us to sit somewhere else. Ma stared straight ahead and ignored me the whole time. When it was time to get off the train, she held me by my wrist and dragged me onto the platform. I complained the whole way home. I complained through dinner. I complained during my bath. I stomped into my bedroom, slammed the door, desperately wishing for a different mother.

Ma came in a few minutes later. She didn't turn on the lights. She sat at the foot of the bed facing me, lit a cigarette, and slowly and dramatically told me about the umbrella. The light from the window filtered through the smoke, making her look like a disembodied head floating in fog. I was terrified. By the time she got to the part about the feng shui master, I had scrambled over to her end of the bed and buried myself in her lap. She just kept talking and smoking. And when the closet door opened and the children appeared, I stopped caring about my bracelet. Fuck the bracelet. Fuck everything you find that doesn't belong to you. I'd rather not be mauled by dirty hungry ghost children in my own bed.

This was the Squawking Chicken's lesson, one she repeated to me over and over again when I was growing up: what's not yours will never be yours. Taking what's not yours can have tragic, frightening consequences.

Ma did not want me to grow up with envy. She didn't want me to grow up wanting what I couldn't have and, more importantly, taking what I didn't earn. Ma wanted me to learn that life wasn't easy, that the things you desire don't just appear one day on the sidewalk, waiting to be picked up, that things are never free. And if they seem free at the beginning, you'll end up paying for them in the end. If you're lucky, she warned, you can write a check, and it'll all even out. If you're not lucky, well, a ghost just might come along and possess your soul.

∂⊙

The Curse of the West Tile

I come from a family of master mah-jong players. My grandmother ran a mah-jong den out of her apartment. As a teenager my mother was beating veterans of the game several decades older than her. The joke in my family is that I was delivered on a mah-jong table—Ma went into labor and just pushed me out in between hands. By the time I was four years old, I could accurately identify every mah-jong tile in a set. There are 144 of them.

Mah-jong is played by the winds: East, South, West and North. Each player is assigned a "wind" position at the beginning of every round. There are four cycles per round, one for each wind. The presence of the "winds," an element of nature, gives mah-jong a certain mysticism that other card games don't have. It is a game governed by luck. For Chinese people, luck is a spiritual property with a personality and its own set of mysterious laws. Sometimes playing mah-jong feels like magic, especially when you're on a roll. Sometimes no matter how thoroughly the tiles are shuffled, you'll keep getting the same hands in the same order, like they're following you, like they're attached to you, telling you what decisions to make. And if you're paying attention, you're winning.

Once I was watching Ma play while sitting on her lap. She was on a hot streak and didn't want me to move and disturb her luck. Ma is a beautiful mah-jong player. As a child, I was mesmerized watching her play. It was those nails. The way she'd reach out with them on the board to select a tile was super glamorous and sexy. She'd pause her forefinger and her third finger on the top of her designated tile, her beautifully glossy red tabs posed side by side like an ad for the perfect manicure, like miniature versions of the tiles themselves, before gently curving them around the block, lifting it so that her thumb could slide below, across the grooves that identified exactly which card she had chosen. Expert mah-jong players don't have to look at a tile to know what it is. They can feel it from the markings against the pads of their thumbs. (While some people inherit recipes from their mothers, the Squawking Chicken passes on her mah-jong tips.)

That day, though, Ma didn't have to even touch the tiles to know which ones they were. Before her turn, every time, she'd tell me what was coming up. If she called for the eight of circles, the eight of circles would arrive. If she called for the six of sticks, it would be the six of sticks that appeared in her hand. This continued for hours, well after I fell asleep in her arms dreaming of my own future mah-jong-queen days, and being able to predict tiles, a veritable gambling Nostradamus.

Given the air of the supernatural that surrounds mah-jong, there are certain unofficial rules that accompany the game. Respected players abide by a mah-jong code of conduct, especially to eliminate suspicion that they're cheating. Cheaters often use shady, dark-side behaviors to gain advantage. Some might intentionally wear a ripped piece of clothing, cleverly hidden, while they're at the table to gain the favor of the benevolent (but often gullible) gambling gods who might mistakenly assume they're poor and need the money. You never want to be the cheater gambling on the Squawking Chicken's territory. Once Ma dropped a tile and when she bent over to pick it up, she noticed that the woman sitting beside her had a tear in her pant leg that looked deliberate. The woman was chased out of there immediately with a chicken feather duster (common in Chinese homes). Ma went door to door to every mah-jong den in town the next day telling everyone about the woman's fraud.

She was made to feel so unwelcome, she ended up emigrating to Australia. Cheaters will be exiled!

Reading at the table is also a cheating technique, albeit an amateur one. This was an expensive lesson for me in college, where I used to play all-night mah-jong with the Chinese students in my dorm. One evening I was up large. The boy sitting across from me, Tommy, was down my share. It is customary to keep playing if the person who has lost the most insists on continuing. Tommy wanted to keep going but left to go up to his room in between rounds. When he came back he had a magazine with him. The word for "magazine" in Chinese is the same as the word for "book." And the word for "book" sounds exactly like the word for "lose." Tommy read his "book" while we played. And I started losing. I lost everything and more. I ended up losing my month's rent.

The next morning I called Ma, my mah-jong guru, to tell her that I got my ass kicked. Up to that point, in my short mah-jong career, I had never, ever lost that badly. Because I'm good. I'm so good at the game that even on days when luck is not with me, I can limit my losses with skill. After all, playing mah-jong is my family's singular talent. So it was shameful that I had been beaten so badly. *What had happened?*

Ma asked me to describe in detail the moment that my streak started shifting. She wanted to know about the patterns of the tiles I was getting and how I interpreted and played them. I had forgotten to mention Tommy's "book" until she pressed me for more information about the person who took my money. When I finally told her about how he was reading during his comeback, she sucked on her teeth, let out an *"Aiya!"* (kind of like saying "Oh my God"), and informed me that I'd been had. Remember, the word for "book" sounds exactly like the word for "lose," and "reading" and "watching" share the same character in Chinese. So when Tommy was reading his magazine he was also "watching me lose." And lose I did. It's a junior move, and it would have never worked on the Squawking Chicken, but it worked on me—just that one time!

Tommy's trickery is considered mah-jong black magic. Mah-jong magic is like the Force in *Star Wars*—there's a good side, the one that flows through the deserving player, and a dark side that can haunt the players who are tempted to use it.

Before I was allowed to play mah-jong with adults, I was trained on tables with my cousins, who were all around the same age. When I was ten years old, I was engrossed in a game after dinner one night. Ma was finishing up her meal and occasionally checking in on me to give me pointers.

Cousin Jin threw out the West tile. The West tile in a mah-jong set is the one that carries the most powerful dark mah-jong magic. Next was Cousin Wai. He threw out a West tile too. Cousin Ling also had a West tile, and she discarded hers. It was my turn. I happened to have a West tile in my hand. Given that the three other West tiles were already exposed, there was no need to keep mine since I'd no longer be able to make a pair. I reached for my West tile just as my ma came up behind me.

She shouted at me so loudly not to toss the West tile that everyone jumped and the tiles scattered all over the floor, the West tile still in my hand.

Why the drama?

Ma gathered the four of us around the kitchen table to explain the Curse of the West Tile. Four West tiles are never to be consecutively thrown out during a mah-jong game. It is mah-jong's most important rule and it is strictly observed.

Ma told the legend of four people who played mah-jong together regularly. One of the players was particularly greedy. Three West tiles were already on the board, discarded in a row, when it came his turn. As luck would have it, he was in possession of the last West tile. The other players pleaded with him not to do it, to wait for the next cycle, for a break in the pattern. But if he kept the West tile, it would screw up his hand. And in getting rid of the West tile, he'd be "calling." "Calling" is the term for a hand that is ready to be won, a hand that is only one short of making a complete set. The man's hand was big on points. It would win him a huge pot. He couldn't wait.

He threw out the West tile. The pot was his. He went home that night the only winner.

A few mornings later, one of his fellow players left home to go to work. She pressed the button for the elevator. The elevator arrived. She stepped inside. As soon as the door closed the cable snapped. The elevator crashed to the bottom and she was killed instantly. It was called a freak accident.

About a month later, one of the other players went to a nightclub. She was on the dance floor when a fight broke out. Bottles were being thrown around so she went to hide behind the bar. The mirror behind the bar was shattered from the altercation. They later found her body when the authorities arrived, a triangular piece of glass sticking out of her neck. It was called a freak accident.

Two players remained.

They met up in a panic. They tried to reassure themselves that it was just coincidence. The player who threw out the fourth West tile tried to convince his sole surviving friend that there was no way the curse was true. He insisted that they would be fine.

That night, while his friend was walking home in the

rain, a burst of lightning struck a lamppost just as he was passing underneath it. The lightning severed the power lines, which then came swinging down. The third mah-jong player was electrocuted and died. It was called a freak accident.

When the fourth West-tile player heard about the accident, he knew he was in deep shit. He went to the temple to pray for guidance, shaking fortune sticks, hoping for a positive message. Every stick that fell to the ground portended calamity. He visited a feng shui master who took one look at him and shut the door in his face. Other feng shui masters refused to see him at all until, finally, a feng shui master from the old village agreed to let him inside. The player begged and begged for advice, for any suggestion, a protective charm or spell that would absolve him of his mistake.

The feng shui master shook his head. "You must account for your avarice. Three lives have been taken because you chose a temporary win over camaraderie and peace. This debt must be paid. It cannot be avoided. You would be wise to embrace your fate so that you can start your next life even, all square."

The player was angry. He refused to accept his judgment. Days passed, then weeks. Nothing happened. The player grew more confident. He even started sleeping again. And when months went by, he believed he was in the clear. He found a new group of people to play mah-jong with.

He continued to win. He won so much he decided to buy himself a new car. It had been half a year since the night he threw out the fourth West tile. On his way home, he decided to drive his new car over a bridge at top speed. When he came off the ramp, he lost control and slammed into a pillar, dead. When they pulled him from the wreckage, there wasn't a bruise on his body, and no blood. But his hand was missing. It was the hand that had thrown the fourth West tile.

Ma's story has prejudiced me against the West tile for life. I even feel weird winning on the West tile and sometimes go out of my way to engineer my cards so that it will never have to work out that way.

When we were driving home that night, I asked Ma why the West tile was so bad.

"It's not the West tile that's bad. It's the people who abuse it who are bad."

Through the West tile story, Ma was teaching me about greed and selfishness. The player who discarded the West tile jeopardized the lives of his friends for the pleasure of a temporary victory. He put his own interests before others. He allowed greed to dominate his decisions. In doing so, he not only affected his own fate, but altered the destiny of his friends. Ma explained that the choices we make are like circles that grow wider, engulfing the people who share our spaces. Greed and selfishness are the attributes of those who believe that life is singular and not inclusive. Ma had seen the effects of greed and selfishness when she was growing up. She'd suffered for the greed and selfishness of her parents, heavy gamblers who consistently put their needs and compulsions over the interests of their children, even willing to risk sacrificing their first daughter for self-preservation.

This is why Ma has always been able to manage her own gambling. Not that she didn't play mah-jong when I was growing up. She was at mah-jong—a lot. But mah-jong never became an obstacle to my education or my well-being. Somehow the Chinese Squawking Chicken managed to turn mah-jong, a game that had had a negative impact on her childhood, into an instructional tool for her own parental philosophy. "You want to screw up your life, that's fine," Ma always said. "The problem is that when you screw up, more often than not, you take other people down with you."

‌

The Ghosts in the Hospital

In Western society, a hospital is for healing. It's where you are taken care of, fixed, protected. A hospital is where life begins. A hospital is also where many lives end. And this is why many Chinese believe hospitals are haunted.

Ma is very familiar with hospitals—too familiar. She's never had the strongest constitution. And when Ma is in the hospital, she has very strict conditions about when I can visit her. No matter how sick she is, she doesn't want me there during certain phases of the moon, when my luck is either too low or too high. She also prefers that I visit her when the sun is still up. And when there are extenuating circumstances that require me to be there in the evening, she insists that I leave before dark. That way I won't be susceptible to the ghosts that linger in the hospital, wandering the halls in the darkness, looking to either latch on to new opportunities or punish those who are still breathing when they can't. Ma worries that the spirits will affect my luck. If I'm on a bad luck streak, she doesn't want to expose me to a situation that could make it worse. If I'm on a good luck streak, she doesn't want to expose me to a situation that could throw off my good run.

A couple of years ago, we were together one afternoon when she complained about not being able to see properly. Her arm was also tingling. This had been going on for a few days. I had to go to a meeting so I urged her to go to the hospital. She was still waiting in the emergency room when my meeting was over. By this time the sun had set. Ma knew I wanted to rush over to be with her but she also remembered that I was leaving the next day on an important work trip. She said I should stay back, at least until the doctors had seen her. An hour passed and I hadn't heard from her, so I rang her cell phone. There was no answer and I started to panic. Finally, my dad called to tell me that they'd determined that Ma had had a mini-stroke. Crying, I started getting my things together, ready to get in the car to go to the hospital. I could hear Dad telling her that I was on my way. It was almost midnight.

She squawked.

And suddenly that voice was shouting me down over the phone. She wouldn't let me come. She refused to listen to my pleas. She was concerned about my career and how it would be affected should I come into some kind of contact with negative spirits at the hospital. The way she was raging at me on the other end of the line, adamant that I stay away, you wouldn't know she'd just had a mini-stroke. No matter how I begged, she would not be swayed. She'd rather not see me than risk me having my luck stolen by spirits.

Ma had had her own experience with hospital spirits.

Once, after a long illness that affected her muscles, she was a patient for several weeks at a rehabilitation hospital. With daily baths and regular wear and tear, her patient wristband had become frayed. Ma kept harassing the staff to give her a new one. Even in the hospital, Ma cared about appearances. She didn't want to have something tattered on her arm. She wanted something new and shiny. Understandably, the nurses were busy, too tied up to make her a fresh wristband and told her to be patient, that she should continue wearing her old one until they could provide her with a replacement. Ma ripped it off and threw it out. She didn't think anyone would have a problem identifying her anyway.

Late that night she felt something pinching her toes on both feet. The pinching became pulling. It didn't hurt, but it was annoying. And persistent. As soon as she started dozing off, the pinching sensation would wake her up again. She slept terribly that night. It happened for three nights in a row and each night, the pinching grew more and more intense, and more annoying. Ma called for the neurologists to come to see her. They ran some tests but could find no medical reason for the toe-pinching sensation that was happening in the middle of the night. In fact, as far as they could tell, her health was improving and her nerves were regenerating.

Ma was puzzled. She was relieved to hear she was getting better but she still needed to know why her feet were getting pinched. She needed an explanation for the feeling she couldn't shake. That she was . . . unwelcome. And she was starting to dread bedtime. Rest was critical to the steady progress she was making and she desperately wanted to get well enough to go home. Ma was still worrying about it when the nurse came into her room for the final vitals check of the day. And she came with a gift.

They'd finally gotten around to printing off a new wristband for her. She put it on and slept uninterrupted that night. Ma realized the next morning that she'd made a mistake by ripping off her original wristband. She was convinced that it was ghosts who had bothered her at night, pinching her feet. The Chinese believe that ghosts are territorial. These particular ghosts must have thought her an intruder because she wasn't wearing a wristband to identify that she belonged at the hospital. Ma determined that the ghosts, zealous about guarding their own turf, had decided she was trespassing until she replaced the wristband, which signified that she was a proper resident of the facility.

Ma had been taught a lesson. She had not only flouted the hospital's policies and procedures, she had done so out of vanity. It was a learning experience for her because Ma had always been kind of . . . shall we say, *selective* about which customs and conventions she'd observe.

For Ma, department stores and flea markets are interchangeable. If you can bargain at a flea market, you should be able to bargain at the mall. "No tax?" is her favorite question. And she will try it anywhere. "Under the table" is her preferred method of payment. Ma also doesn't believe in queuing for anything. On weekends Dad and I, for years now, will find an excuse to not arrive with her at a dim sum restaurant if there's a waiting list because Ma just sits down wherever there's an open table. She does it so authoritatively she never gets questioned. By the time Dad and I get there a few minutes later, the teapot will already be on the table and she'll have ordered.

Ma usually gets away with this behavior. Except for the time when the ghosts called her out for not adhering to patient identification policy. And it made her re-evaluate her approach to order. At least at the hospital. But to this day, her favorite question is, "No tax?"

Wise Man Shou and the Peach

Chinese people believe that pregnant women attract ghosts. Those who've died prematurely, and without closure, are always looking to come back. We call them *yoon gwai*, or "clinging spirits"; they yearn to return to the land of the living, loitering in the space between life and beyond, like gamblers who've lost everything but still can't leave the casino, choosing instead to stand around the poker table watching other people play, desperate for a chance to get back into the game.

For the *yoon gwai*, the chance to get back into the game is by process of *tao toi*. The expression literally translated means "jump into the womb," the Chinese version of reincarnation. The vessels are unborn children whose souls in the womb remain pristine and unformed, perfect. In the competitive unborn child department, Ma was carrying the most perfect one, a baby every ghost wanted to inhabit, the ultimate *tao toi* candidate. While my birth was unremarkable, my ma's pregnancy was extraordinary.

The *yoon gwai* could only affect Ma when she was asleep, which is why she had such terrible dreams when she was expecting me. They haunted her every night for months. They followed her into dark alleys and backed her into damp corners, reaching toward her belly with their decomposed fingers, sometimes on their knees, begging to be born again through her. She said they bargained and cajoled. They told tragic stories: one girl was betrayed by a lover who pushed her off a cliff so that he'd be free to marry a rich girl for her fortune; another man was poisoned in the night by his brother who wanted to take over his business; there was a boy, no more than six, with no fingers and only thumbs who'd hook them into her pockets and beg for the opportunity to live a different kind of life. They wailed at her in her nightmares, inching closer and closer to take her baby, and Ma would sacrifice herself every time. Her subconscious suicide was the ultimate act of parental selflessness—and she'd wake up in the middle of the night, just before stabbing herself, my eternal hero and savior. It was this remarkable courage that caught the attention of the Old Wise Man.

Have you ever been in a Chinese home? In addition to the ceramic cat with one fist in the air, most Chinese homes display statues of the Three Wise Men.

Fu's the dude on the left. He's for Good Luck. Lu is in the middle. He brings Prosperity. And the ancient one with no hair holding a staff in one hand and a peach in the other, a Gandalf of the East, is Shou, who represents Long Life.

The ghosts were especially persistent the night before Ma went into labor. *Pick me! Pick me!* they cried, surrounding her on all sides, clutching at her hair, her nightgown, greedily eyeing her stomach; she was petrified, too afraid to act. And then suddenly they shrank in fear. Old Wise Man Shou, with his benevolent smile and kind eyes, had come to rescue her.

Shou waved the ghosts away and helped Ma to her feet. He told her not to be afraid. He told her he was there to protect her, and that she deserved his protection because she was so appreciative, respectful and brave. Then he gave her his peach. *Eat this*, he said. *It will keep your baby safe.* Ma protested, claiming that she did not feel worthy. Wise Man Shou insisted and blessed her humble nature.

I will come back for my fruit once you no longer need it. Take care of your daughter. And then he hobbled away slowly. Ma woke up. She knew she was having a girl. And she was in labor.

A friend once asked me why an old Chinese lady at the park gave her the evil eye while she was walking by her with her newborn. Chinese custom dictates that a child must pass his or her "full moon" before leaving the home, otherwise it's very bad luck, for both the baby and the mother. After a month of seclusion, there's a great celebration to mark the baby's introduction to society. I cried and cried at my first-moon party. Ma said people were whispering that it was a

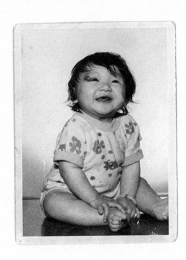

bad omen and the gossipy aunties and neighborhood rumor-mongers suspected that she'd given birth to a curse. The next morning when Ma picked me up out of my crib, she noticed a small red dot on the corner of my right eyelid. Initially she thought it must have been because I was crying so hard the night before. But the red dot continued to grow, week after week. By the time I turned one, it had become a large red mass, with a faint line through the middle. It was the color of a ripe peach and, Ma says, in the shape of one too, although in photographs it looks more like a yin-yang symbol to me.

Specialists from around the world flew in to look at my eye-peach. Every week my parents took me to appointments. The doctors said it was a medical anomaly and, in the end, they told my parents that if they operated, there was a strong possibility there could be nerve damage and I could lose my eyesight. So my parents decided to leave it. It just added to Ma's resolve. She had the courage and the character to raise a daughter with a freak spot on her face.

When I was four, my eye-peach started to get smaller. Back we went to the doctors, and again, week after week, they'd measure the gradually shrinking peach and shake their heads, flummoxed by its sudden retreat. This is when Ma remembered Wise Man Shou and her dream. Wise Man Shou was taking back his peach. It/He had protected me through the worst, and now I was ready to go on without his stewardship. By the time I turned six, the eye-peach was barely noticeable, a very faint pink shadow but only if you looked closely.

And yet, it lives on. Ma believes the eye-peach not only guarded me from spirits, but it also must have blocked illness and disease. I was rarely sick as a child, if at all, because Wise Man Shou's gift inoculated me against what could have been a deadly infection, or maybe even a devastating accident. Wise Man Shou's gift, however, was only given as a direct result of Ma's protective love.

So it turns out that I'm Harry Potter. Except not. There's no seven-book series dedicated to my legend because from the very beginning of the story of my life, I have always been a supporting character. The Squawking Chicken is the leading lady.

Most children's stories mythologize the child—the children are golden, special, chosen. And most parents mythologize their children, making their children the stars of the show, the focus of the attention as they lurk just offstage, eagerly accepting any leftover warmth from the lights that are positioned to shine primarily on the protagonists, their sons and daughters, settling for the small credit that comes occasionally for creating these extraordinary creatures.

For the Chinese Squawking Chicken, *she* was the extraordinary creature. She mythologized herself. The legend of my eye-peach had nothing to do with me and everything to do with her—her remarkable courage in the face of the ghosts, her profound love. She did for me what her parents didn't do for her: she was my mother and my hero; she gave me life by saving me from the ghosts. And she taught me to spend the rest of my life paying her back.

These sound like tall tales, I know. Entertaining but improbable, the kind of stories a child outgrows when her world becomes bigger. And yet, I haven't outgrown the Squawking Chicken's stories. I hear the conviction in her voice when she tells them. She tells them because she believes them. And because she believes them, I go on believing them. Such is the power of my mother's storytelling—for me it has been greater than reason, stronger than doubt, more enduring than fact. The moral messages embedded in Ma's stories form the foundation of my life code and standard of conduct. Nothing could be more real.

Fittingly then, the Squawking Chicken's best ghost story is also the one that was meant to teach me her most important lesson: Mother loves best, Mother knows best.

CHAPTER 3

Where's My Money?

Every year on my ma's birthday, I call to wish her happy birthday. Every year on *my* birthday, I call *her* to wish *myself* happy birthday. Ma does not call me on my birthday. I am expected to call *her*. There's a reason for this, of course, and I'll never forget it, obviously, but some years, for fun, I'll ask her why, just to hear her say it again.

"Why should I call you on your birthday? You should call *me* on your birthday. To thank me for giving birth to you. Now where's my money?"

There is no better way to demonstrate gratitude for Ma giving birth to me than to give her money. If it's not the first thing she says when she sees me, it's definitely the second thing out of my ma's mouth when she sees me: "Where's my money?"

It's a question that many Western parents might find appalling. How could a mother hit up her kid for cash, and so blatantly? Growing up in North America, I've learned that money is an uncomfortable subject for most people. It's considered bad form to talk money. It's considered in poor taste to discuss how much things cost, how much you paid for something, how much you are paid to work. Many of my friends who did not grow up in immigrant households never discussed money with their parents. They never knew how much their parents earned. They were unaware of mortgages and expenses. Their parents treated money as a taboo subject.

Chinese families, however, are generally more open about money. Much has been made in the media about the growth of Chinese materialism after the 2008 U.S. stock market crash and subsequent recession. As China continues to rise as an economic superpower, business analysts and cultural anthropologists have noted the Chinese consumer's seemingly insatiable appetite for luxury items. Many Chinese people are not shy about throwing around their cash and telling you about it afterward. It's the second part of the sentence that makes us different, not the first. In my opinion, Chinese people aren't more materialistic; it's just that we're more candid about our materialism.

In Chinese culture, money is directly connected to respect and love. Money is how we demonstrate our gratitude.

Money is how we show we care. Money is an uncomplicated symbol of feeling. It is more tangible than a hug, it is more useful than a kiss, and often longer lasting. Most importantly, money is *helpful*. And between parent and child, between family members and friends, it is dispensed in this spirit. This is evident in most of our customs and traditions. This is why elders gift the young with red paper envelopes called *lai see* stuffed with money on birthdays and holidays. *Lai see* means "lucky money." So the money does double duty—its primary function is obvious, but it also comes with good vibes and wishes to keep you safe and happy.

When my cousins and I were growing up, we'd be disappointed at Christmas if our pile of boxed presents under the tree was particularly bountiful. Too many presents meant that we'd be receiving fewer *lai see*, and everyone preferred *lai see* to regular gifts. I can buy my own sweater, thank you very much, with the money you give me and, frankly, I'd rather buy candy. After dinner, when we were allowed to open our presents, we'd always gather at the very end to count our cash. My grandmother on my father's side was the most generous. She gave ten bucks at a time. Ten bucks bought a lot of gummy bears.

Lai see is the standard at Chinese weddings too. We don't mess around with a registry. And we have no use for a gravy boat anyway. There's your tip for the next time you're invited to a Chinese wedding. Take whatever it costs to buy a gravy boat and shove it in an envelope with a card. I promise you it will be more appreciated.

The subject of money comes up a lot at a Chinese wedding. One of my favorite traditions at a Chinese wedding is the Bride Bargain. It is customary for the bride and groom to arrive at the ceremony together. But, beforehand, the groom, along with his crew, picks the bride up at her home. He knocks on the door. The bride does not answer. Instead, she waits inside while the bridesmaids negotiate their fee to allow the groom access, shouting through the door. The denominations always involve the number nine. The number nine traditionally represents longevity. In other words, the more nines, the longer the marriage.

The game is played like a proper business transaction. The groom and his posse start low: *We'll give you nine dollars and ninety-nine cents.* The bridesmaids reply: *That's it? No way! We won't take any less than nine million, nine hundred and ninety-nine thousand, and ninety-nine cents!*

And they'll go back and forth for a while until they arrive at a figure that makes everyone happy. At that point, a bridesmaid unlocks the door so the groom can pass the cash through, and once the girls are finished counting the bills, he storms in to collect his bride. The money is then split among the bridesmaids and is meant as a thank-you gift for their years of support and friendship.

From there, the bride and groom head over to their parents' for a tea ceremony where they both kneel before their elders, offering tea with their heads bowed. In return for the tea, the older generation gives the couple their wedding *lai see*. The *lai see* represents the head start that the parents and grandparents can provide to their children and their well-wishes for a long and happy marriage.

At my wedding, Ma told me not to spend my *lai see,* but to tuck it into my pillowcase instead. For more than ten years now, I've been literally shoving *lai see* in my pillowcase, where it's been accumulating as I sleep, a fertile place to nurture the well-wishes and hopes from my parents and, of course, my bank account. The *lai see* in the pillow symbolizes personal wealth and the idea is that as the pillowcase grows, so does your overall prosperity. And I've needed it too. Because the day I became a wife was the day my parents were not only no longer responsible for me, it was also the day I officially became responsible to them, financially at least. The flow of money changed direction. And Ma is getting more and more expensive.

Most people take their parents out for dinner for their birthdays. This is normal, right? After I got married and as I was becoming more established in my career, I graduated from the birthday phone call to the birthday party. Now that I have a career and a steady income, it's expected that I not only pay for Ma, but also for everyone in her Chinese opera class and her Buddhist prayer circle (even if they don't really know each other all that well).

Every year, Ma celebrates her birthday with a party. She books out several tables at a Chinese restaurant and the private room too. She and her guests start at lunch with dim sum. After dim sum, they move over to the private room for several hours of mah-jong. Then they come back out for dinner. The best food is ordered: suckling pig, Peking duck, lobster, crab—basically the kind of elaborate menu served at a Chinese wedding, only every year, on March 9, it's like Ma is remarrying herself and sending me the bill.

Ma doesn't front like she's the person paying for her party though. She makes it very clear to everyone there that I'm the one who's treating her and her friends. It's impossible to sign for it discreetly, and besides, I never pay for her birthday with a credit card anyway. Chinese establishments prefer cash. And Ma prefers that I pay cash. She's always on me about it in the days leading up to the event.

"Don't forget to bring cash. Best to bring twenties."

"Why twenties?"

"It takes longer to pay in twenties. You have to count out your bills."

Here's how it goes down: After dessert, she'll tell the staff that we're ready to settle. They'll present her with the check. She and Dad will inspect every line item to make sure they weren't ripped off and that the 10-percent-off special was applied. Ma never eats anywhere Chinese unless she gets a discount. (I have no idea how she gets this discount. All I know is that by the time she brings me to whatever new Chinese restaurant she's hot on at the moment, the discount is always in place and they always know her by name. Once I tried asking her whether or not she felt gross about eating her food at a discount. She told me that things taste better when they come as a deal.)

Once my parents are pleased with the check, Ma will make a big production out of passing it to me, announcing to all her guests that I'll be the one paying for it. Which is my cue to pull out my wallet with a smile on my face, as forty or so pairs of eyes are watching, and take out my stack of twenties, counting them out one by one. The first time I did this I had performance anxiety. That's exactly what it is—a performance, the performance of paying for Ma's birthday dinner, playing the part of the generous, dutiful daughter. That first time my hands were unsteady and when two bills were stuck together I wasn't very graceful in pulling them apart; they were wrinkled by the time I laid them down on the table. Ma criticized me afterward for my lack of coordination. She said that people who are magnanimous about paying do so smoothly and elegantly, and that I looked stingy and unwilling. Maybe unconsciously. It was a lot of money. My skills improved the following year. I know this because she didn't mention it again.

The birthday-party-paying ceremony is an annual opportunity for Ma to show off. Her showing off, however, is not limited to her birthday parties and, therefore, my paying for things is not limited to her birthdays either.

I always know when Ma is calling me with an audience. For starters, she always sounds nice when she's talking to me in front of other people. When I say "nice," I mean strained. It's an effort for my ma to modulate that squawking chicken noise into something she thinks sounds sweet but really sounds like she's choking out her words. One day she called me when she was out with her friends. "Daughter, I told all the aunties at Chinese opera class that you are buying me a cruise and now they all want to come too! We are going to Europe!"

I never offered to send her on a cruise. Not exactly. We were on the phone the night before and she was complaining about how long it had been since she'd been back to Hong

Kong and even though SARS had passed over a couple of years before, in 2003, she was still afraid of going there. So I told her she should go to Europe, go on holiday with Dad. She said she didn't want to go to Europe because it was hard to get around and the languages would screw her up. So I told her it'd be easier for her if she went on a cruise because that way there would be a set schedule. She said she'd think about it.

Not even twenty-four hours later, she not only had thought about it, I was now paying for it. I stayed on the phone silently and let her finish our conversation. She answered questions I didn't ask. *Oh, daughter, that's okay. Mommy will take care of her own insurance, you don't have to worry about that. Yes, daughter, I will make sure to tell you exactly how much it is so that you can call the travel agent. No, daughter, I don't have to fly first class. The aunties and I will all fly together.*

When I hung up, my husband asked me if Ma was talking to me in front of her friends again. He was used to it by then. But it had been strange for him at the beginning, as it would be for those growing up in non-Chinese households. For an outsider, the automatic assumption here would be that my ma is greedy and opportunistic, taking advantage of her daughter's resources for selfish gain, vanity and ego.

But my parents don't need the money. They've worked hard. They can afford to pay for their own birthday parties.

And everyone at the party knows my parents can afford to pay for the birthday party. My paying for her birthday parties isn't about exploitation. Rather, my paying for the birthday party is about honor. My paying for Ma's parties is a very public honor. It is a demonstration of honor to the community. It's a manifestation of one of the most important concepts in Chinese society: Filial Piety.

That children should be good to their parents is a common expectation across all cultures. In Chinese culture, children *have* to be good to their parents. For the Chinese, Filial Piety is considered the fundamental cornerstone of an enlightened civilization. It is the original building block of Confucian philosophy and therefore the defining virtue in Chinese culture: our primary objective in life is to respect our parents and our ancestors. It is, according to Confucius, the only way to ensure peace and happiness for future generations.

Filial Piety then dictates every action. We must care for our parents inside and outside the home. We must work hard to support the home. We must sacrifice for the home. Not for a day, not for a year, but *forever.* Filial Piety is a lifelong requirement. It is every child's duty to respect the parent, to support the parent, and to bring pride and honor to the parent. Filial Piety puts the onus on the child and not the parent.

This is the critical difference between Chinese and Western parenting philosophy. Modern Western parenting emphasizes the child over the parent. Being a parent is widely accepted as the most selfless of human acts. A mother wants only the best for her child—to provide opportunities for her child to achieve *her* dreams, to accomplish *her* goals, to live *her* best life possible—with no reward in return. A child is encouraged to pursue her own objectives independently. The parent is happy if the child is happy. According to the tenets of Filial Piety, however, the situation is reversed: a child can only achieve true happiness when she has successfully secured the happiness of her parents. And this has always been my ma's position as a parent. It was also her position when she was a child.

Ma's parents weren't particularly responsible or loving. They compromised her repeatedly. They were neglectful and unsupportive. And worse still, they showed no remorse. By Western standards, it would have been well within Ma's rights to turn her back on her parents. To forsake them and not forgive. To abandon them without regret. But while Ma survived her ordeal and became stronger for it, finding her squawking chicken voice because of it, she continued to observe the principles of Filial Piety. She never spoke ill of her parents outside the home. She continued to play the part of dutiful first daughter. She continued to look after her five brothers and sisters without complaint. She handed over a majority of her earnings to her parents without resentment. When she married my father, she kneeled humbly before the village, in the presence of her ancestors, to thank her parents for raising her. And she kept bailing them out of trouble, over and over and over again, often at her own expense.

I spent the summer before my sixth birthday in Hong Kong with Ma. Every other day she'd take me to my grandmother's to check in. One afternoon, there was debris littered along the corridor leading up to my grandmother's apartment where she ran a mah-jong den. The door was already open. It was a mess when we stepped inside. There was glass everywhere. The television had been smashed and was lying on the floor. Mah-jong tiles were all over the place. The couch had been slashed. I remember slipping on a chopstick, my mother catching me by the arm before my head hit the corner of the coffee table. My grandmother was wailing in the bathtub. My grandfather was chain-smoking in the bedroom, the door closed.

It turns out Grandmother had been playing high-stakes mah-jong at one of the bigger mah-jong dens in town. She was carrying big losses and was behind on her payments. The mah-jong dens were run by local gang members and they'd sent some of their thugs to collect. When Grandmother couldn't come up with the cash, they gave her a warning by trashing her apartment. Next time, they warned, they'd come for something more permanent.

Ma knew these were serious threats. She also knew they could not be put off any longer and that the situation was beyond her negotiation skills. Ma took my hand and marched me out the door. We walked to the bank where one of her good friends, Auntie Lai, was the bank manager. She told me to wait outside. I could see her in Auntie's office through the glass, smoking her cigarettes, waiting while Auntie walked back and forth between the teller and the vault. Eventually Ma signed some papers and zipped up her purse. We were on our way to pay off Grandmother's debt. After Ma settled up at the mah-jong den, we headed back to Grandmother's apartment. On the way, she stopped at a toy store and bought me a pop-up card game. I sat on Grandmother's shredded couch, playing my new game, while Ma bathed her mother and put her to bed. I kept playing while Ma picked up the chairs and the overturned tables, while she swept the broken pieces of television into a trash bin, while she mopped the tiles on her hands and knees with a washcloth, her perfect long red nails pushing back and forth, scrubbing the dirt and the dust off the floor.

Two days later, we flew back to Canada, our trip cut

short by a month. Ma went back to work. She was already working two jobs, but she took on an extra job on weekends so she could pay off the loan she'd taken out to save Grandmother's ass.

My ma repaid her mother's debt. She did the same for her father when he fell ill. I was eleven that summer. Grandfather had been ailing for weeks. I was afraid to look at him. His eyes were yellow. His face was yellow. His breath smelled. Grandmother suspended gaming at her mah-jong den. It wasn't fun anymore to go to my grandparents'. Before Grandfather's illness, it was always boisterous over there. The mah-jong players gossiped. They were the entertainment. Now, without them, it was too quiet. Grandfather kept moaning from the bedroom and there was no one to play with, no one to talk to. People had started to write him off, saying it was only a matter of time.

Ma had a doctor of Chinese medicine come over to examine Grandfather, looking for a cure. The man had very long nose hairs. I was hesitant to greet him at the door. Ma scolded me for being rude. They disappeared into Grandfather's bedroom for a long time, so long I started to worry that Ma would have long nose hairs herself when she came back out. When they finally emerged, Ma had that expression on her face I was beginning to recognize—determination. After Dr. Nose Hair left, she picked up the phone to call my auntie Lai, making arrangements to have me stay with her for a few days because she had to go on a trip to help Grandfather. I started crying. I didn't want Ma to take off on me because Dr. Nose Hair told her to.

But Ma was off to Mainland China. She said she was going in search of a magic turtle that could save Grandfather's life. A magic turtle!? This made me rethink the grossness of Dr. Nose Hair. The dude was recommending magic turtles. He couldn't be that bad. Many Chinese believe that turtles have healing properties. Turtle soup is said to be an effective cure for a number of diseases for those who are suffering and a longevity booster for those who are healthy. According to Dr. Nose Hair, the turtles from a small village in the Chinese province of Guangzhou were particularly potent. Ma was to buy a magic turtle from the village, bring it back and prepare it using the recipe that Dr. Nose Hair had prescribed. She told me it would be a rough trip, not suitable for children. I was to hang out at Auntie Lai's until she came home.

It took her two days. She went straight to Grandfather's when she returned. I insisted that Auntie Lai bring me over there because I was so desperate to see the turtle. Unfortunately, it had already been killed and taken apart and was boiling by the time I got back. Ma was standing over a steaming terra-cotta pot and when I rushed forward to look, she shouted at me to get out of her way. Ma's voice was even sharper than usual that day. And she looked tired. She hadn't had time to have her hair blown out. It was lank, parted in the middle, stuck to both sides of her face. I knew not to bother her.

A few hours passed and the magic turtle soup was ready. Ma took a bowl into Grandfather's bedroom. She sat in a chair next to the bed. I was terrified to go inside, but I was also really curious about whether or not the magic turtle would make Grandfather feel better. I peeked my head around the corner and saw Ma's long red fingernails holding up a soup spoon to Grandfather's mouth. His eyes were closed. She patiently waited every time he gulped. I was disgusted by the sounds and the dank stench wafting off his body and, at the same time, fascinated by those nails, that spoon, circling slowly around the bowl, skimming a layer off the top every time, then making its way back to Grandfather's lips.

Ma fed Grandfather every three hours until every drop in the pot had been consumed. Three days later he was able to get out of bed. After a week he was walking around again. Two weeks later he was almost back to normal. The magic turtle totally worked.

Many years later, when Grandmother died, and Grandfather had already passed away, I asked Ma about the debt and the magic turtle incidents. I asked her how she could go to such great lengths to help her parents, especially after the way she'd been treated. Ma explained that Filial Piety protects the future. She believes that Filial Piety is like depositing money in a bank account—the more good you do for your parents, the more bonus karma points you accumulate in your savings. Those savings are there for your own children. So that if perhaps they encounter challenges, or make mistakes, the goodwill, the good karma that's been stored in the Filial Piety Bank Account, can be withdrawn to see them through the hard times, make their trials easier, make their tribulations shorter. Ma was good to her parents for me then. Sort of. More specifically, Ma treated her parents well so that I would eventually treat her well, and make all her efforts worthwhile. This is Ma's particular spin on Filial Piety. Ultimately her application and interpretation of it benefits *her*.

For the Squawking Chicken, being born is a gift—a parent's first gift to their child—and it's a gift that a child must keep repaying, over and over and over again. Ma paid back her parents. And now I'm doing the same.

But is that selfish? Does that mean she's a selfish person? Well, sure. Aren't all parents selfish though? Honestly, aren't they?

Why do people have children?

People have children to have someone to love. People have children because their children make *them* happy.

Is that selfless, or is it selfish?

For my ma, the decision was selfish. And she owns it. She had me to make her happy. In her mind, why would she go to such lengths to carry around a baby, to feed it, to worry about it, to hope for it if, in some measure, she would not be getting something out of it? This way of thinking is particularly effective in managing a rebellious teenager's entitlement and outrage when mandated to follow household rules.

ᗞᗡ

When I was sixteen my curfew was one o'clock for special occasions (birthday parties, etc.). This was not negotiable. There was an upcoming school dance I was really excited about. I had a boyfriend. He was popular, and because I was his girlfriend, I was popular too. The dance was the first off-site school event of the year where we would show up as a couple. A lot of other girls were jealous of me. So I really wanted to look great that night. I wanted to walk in holding hands with my boyfriend and live up to the envy. My dress was really cute. My hair was working for me too. And all the cool kids were going to a house party afterward. The plan was to make out in the basement and stay out until dawn. I was convinced that my experience wouldn't be complete if I had to be home by one o'clock and skipped the after-party. Besides, I had to be there to make sure no one else would hit on my boyfriend.

I waited until Ma was in a great mood. A few days before the dance, she came home from mah-jong after a lucky night. So I asked her before bed if we could make an exception. If I could stay out late after the dance to hang out with my friends. She said no. So I switched tactics. I told her that if I didn't go, I would be an outcast, and people wouldn't want to be friends with me. Big mistake. That only strengthened her resolve. "Why should I made adjustments to the rules just because you're insecure?" she asked.

I decided to regroup and try again later. I was expecting a test result back the next day anyway. And Ma usually rewarded me for good marks. When I came home from school that afternoon, I showed her my test score. It was 93 percent. "Look, Ma, I got one of the highest marks in class. As a bonus, can we extend my curfew after the dance?"

"Why should I extend your curfew when it's so obviously working and you're doing so well in school? What if I extend your curfew and you start failing? No thank you."

So I lost it. I railed and I raged. I threw down an epic

teenage tantrum. I accused her of child abuse. I told her I hated her. I said she was the worst mother of anyone I knew. I told her she sucked at being a mother. "I don't understand why you even had me when all you ever do is make me miserable. Why did you bring me into this world?!"

These would be hurtful words to hear for some mothers. And some mothers, guilted by their child's unhappiness, would relent. Because they prioritize their children's happiness over their own, and ultimately most parents only want happiness for their kids. Parents are supposed to be selfless. This is how it is with my husband's family. They are Polish. They would never dream of accepting gifts from their children. It feels wrong to be on the receiving end. To them, they should always be the givers. Unlike my ma and her cruise, when we sent my in-laws to Italy for their fortieth wedding anniversary, they desperately wanted to return the favor. They refuse our every gesture to help them, not out of pride, but because of their ethics. They consider it unconscionable for a parent to take from a child. Instead, in many ways, they put themselves at the mercy of their children, forever responsible for their happiness.

My happiness is a priority for my mother only if it leads to her own happiness. Which is why, when I tried to use the threat of my unhappiness as a weapon against her, it never worked. Guilting my ma has never worked. Remember, according to the tenets of Filial Piety, a child achieves true happiness and enlightenment only when she has successfully secured the happiness of her parents. And according to the tenets of my ma's customized brand of Filial Piety, her child's happiness is simply a bonus to securing hers. After all, she earned it: *I brought you into this world and you get to go to school. You get to eat good food. You get to have friends. How lucky you are! How much luckier you are than Old Woman Choi down at the market? When I was growing up, her kids had to eat leftover chicken scraps and they didn't know how to read and write! Why aren't you thanking me that you are not Old Woman Choi? Why aren't you thanking me for your life? I gave you such a good life. I gave you the best life. Did you thank me for your best life? Is this how you thank me for your best life? Is this how you thank me for having a life?*

So I came home at one o'clock. How can you argue with that? Even if I didn't think she gave me the best life, she did actually give me life—the most basic, important gift of all. And in doing so she deserves to be repaid for it. With obedience first . . . and then cash later. Or jewelry. Or cruises.

CHAPTER 4

You Will Be Thanking Me for Your Entire Life

The first time I ever spent my own money on Ma it was for a pair of gold hoop earrings. I was twelve. My parents were divorced. They'd split up just before my seventh birthday and Ma had moved back to Hong Kong and remarried, leaving me in the care of my father. I visited her at Christmas, spring break and on summer holidays.

That year, she'd come back to Canada for a friend's wedding. We were at the mall with some relatives shopping for a wedding gift. I'd just started getting interested in clothes and wanted to buy an expensive dress that was totally impractical. She wouldn't buy it for me so I told her that I wanted to use my *lai see* and birthday money to buy it for myself. She still wouldn't let me because she said it was a stupid use of my savings. Furious and embarrassed to be shut down in front of other people, I told her that she had no right to tell me what

to do since she had bailed on me to fuck off with another man. It was a sucker punch I'd been waiting six years to hit her with.

I had a hard time after my parents' separation. Ma called me regularly after she first left and, every couple of months, a big box would arrive from Hong Kong full of toys and clothing. It would be a year before I saw her again and in that time, I felt her absence inside and outside of our home. I was at that age when parents are actively involved in their children's lives at school. There were parent-teacher conferences. There were recitals and Christmas concerts. Most of the other kids had two people waiting for them at all times. And the few kids whose parents were divorced, like mine, were picked up by their mothers. At that time, in the early eighties, it was socially assumed that all kids had two parents.

On school release forms it was always the word "parents," never the "parent or guardian" phrasing that's become commonplace today. And if any parent was singled out for any reason, it was always the mom. "When you get home tonight, remind your mom that tomorrow is baked goods day for the charity drive so she should pack an extra cookie with you for lunch." Dad was among the first wave of single fathers. And while it's awesome to think of him as a trailblazer now, back then it only made me more different. I was the only Chinese girl in my class. I was the only girl in class with just a dad.

But if it was uncomfortable for Dad to be both father and mother to me during those years, he never let on. He was never late, he was never disorganized, he was always there, a

dutiful father whose love had to fill a Squawking Chicken–sized gap.

So when Ma denied me the dress in the mall that day, my tantrum was part adolescent resentment combined with parental preference. Up to then, my loyalties were with Dad. It felt good to hurt her.

Ma's eyes narrowed. For once, the Squawking Chicken did not squawk. When the Squawking Chicken isn't squawking, she's either almost dead or you know you're in some deep shit. My family members disappeared. Ma turned on her heel, knowing I would follow. She took me to a coffee shop, ordered a cup of coffee, and asked me if I wanted one too. I did. It felt very grown-up. And, indeed, we had a very grown-up conversation. Ma decided to tell me about the history of her relationship with Dad, and why she left him.

Ma had dropped out of school after Grade 10 to support her family. Without a proper education, there was only so much she could do. At first she made money placing bets for people at the track and collecting tips. From there, having made connections with local trading merchants who used to hang out at the gambling halls, she worked for them under the table, organizing shipping orders and schedules for Western

goods to cross on the black market into China. Later on, she got a job at a real estate firm selling overseas property. The commission was great. She booted around in a BMW, bought clothes in Kowloon, traveled throughout Asia and still had enough money to send home every week.

While Ma was a single girl hitting her stride, Dad was just getting started. He was a poor farmer boy from Tsuen Wan, a small town about half an hour away from Yuen Long, the sixth of ten children, shy and unsophisticated. As a boy and through his teen years, he was mentored by a monk who taught him Buddhist scripture and impressed upon him the value of hard work and perseverance. For a while, he considered entering the monastery himself. But meeting Ma changed everything.

Dad had a job at the Yuen Long courthouse as a clerk. His supervisor, Mr. Lai, who would eventually become my godfather, recognized his potential and intended to promote him. Mr. and Mrs. Lai were good friends with the Squawking Chicken. They all played mah-jong together. Ma would occasionally visit Mr. Lai at the courthouse. She'd pull up in her BMW, strut across the office like she owned it, squawking her arrival as if everyone should stop working because she was there. Dad was instantly infatuated. Or, as she put it, "Your daddy couldn't even dream that he'd ever meet someone as amazing as me." Since Dad didn't have the nerve to ask her out, Mr. Lai kept trying to set them up. Ma saw it as a charitable opportunity, a kindness she was bestowing just once on this hillbilly with the glasses and the nerdy clothes.

She wouldn't go out with him again after their first date. The Squawking Chicken had an active social life. She was smart, well connected, popular and well-dressed, and after years of family drama, the situation at home was finally stabilized. She had opportunities. She had plans. And Dad was a total nerd—shy and awkward, he wore goofy clothes and had country manners. "Your daddy only knew how to eat chicken! Only chicken and rice! And my underwear cost more than his entire wardrobe." He didn't fit into her world.

But he refused to be put off. So one night he stood outside her window, across the street so she could see him, from after dinner until morning, just to demonstrate his ardor. People made fun of him as they passed. He looked pathetic— the geek pining for the girl who was out of his league, the clueless loser who couldn't take a hint. It was a John Hughes movie. But it worked. Dad wore her down. He made Ma feel like she was the only woman who mattered, like she was worth fighting for. They fell in love over the objections of her parents who, by this point, had conveniently white-washed their lives. There was no more drinking. There was no more adultery. Her father was now a bus driver. Her mother stayed home to look after Ma's siblings, which basically meant she played mah-jong all day while Ma helped them with their household expenses. Her parents were enjoying her generosity and the fact that she was successful was

making them look good. They were hoping she'd hook up with a rich businessman who could support them too. So when they found out that Ma was dating some hick with bad clothes and no car, they were disappointed. They thought Dad was beneath her, beneath *them*.

But Ma believed in Dad. She knew he was tenacious and hardworking. She encouraged him to pursue night classes and advance through the government employment system. They were married a year after they met and moved into a modest but comfortable apartment in a good neighborhood. They were young and excited and he had a promising career ahead of him. He earned enough so that Ma didn't have to work anymore. She had never been happier.

And then family obligations interfered. Dad's oldest sister, Sue, who was the third child in their family of ten, had immigrated to Canada with her husband. There were fewer opportunities in Hong Kong for his siblings, and many of them were hoping to follow Sue's lead and build their futures overseas. Sue was now settled in Toronto with three children and ready to help other family members. According to my ma, Dad was Sue's favorite brother; she wanted him to come over first, even though my parents had no complaints about staying in Hong Kong. They were better positioned than the rest of Dad's family and weren't looking to relocate. Ma's life was leisurely. When Dad went to work, she'd go for dim sum with her friends and then play mah-jong until it was time for dinner. They had a housekeeper. On weekends, they'd leave for romantic getaways on Lantau Island or Macau, just short ferry rides away. Dad had found his princess and she was introducing him to experiences he never thought he'd have. Ma finally found someone she could trust completely, and he was her family now. But Ma claims that Dad's family, the Luis, believed Sue would be discouraged if Dad turned down her offer, and that she'd be hesitant to extend it to anyone else. Dad felt pressured to follow Sue's lead to go to Canada and Ma didn't fight it. In that generation, women followed their husbands and, besides, Ma was no longer contributing financially to their home. In the end, my parents decided to do what was best for the rest of the family and packed up to go to Canada, to start over in a new country. "I was just twenty-one years old," Ma told me in the coffee shop, still stirring her coffee that had long gone cold, the spoon caught in her long red nails spinning around and around.

Ma went from being a pampered housewife in Hong Kong to working two jobs in Canada. Suddenly she was scrubbing dishes at a restaurant, those nails now chipped and softened, and trying to understand English. Nobody showed her to the best table at dim sum and there were no more afternoon mah-jong games. Nobody recognized her at the grocery store. She had nowhere to go but to work and back, and eventually she even took on a second job waiting tables.

But she had reinvented herself before. She was the phoenix who rose from the ashes of her rape. And her phoenix-like characteristics served her well again here, not unlike many immigrants who find themselves in new countries, shocked by a new culture. She was adaptable. She learned how to drive on the other side of the road. She went about creating a new circle of friends with the local Toronto Chinese community, mah-jong their uniting force. (Ma has a radar for mah-jong. She can sniff out a mah-jong player within a fifteen-block radius.) She and her friends would go shopping for North American goods to send back to Hong Kong, writing to friends and family about her new and thoroughly modern Canadian lifestyle. The Squawking Chicken takes over Canada! No matter how hard it actually was, back home they would never know. Back home the Squawking Chicken's mythology was intact.

I was born two years after my parents' arrival in Toronto. Ma said she knew I'd be a big baby because one day she ate a bowl of cherries and she could feel a new set of stretch marks extending across her belly.

"From the very beginning, Elaine is always wanting more," she likes to repeat, whenever people ask her about how big I was as a baby. "She make my stomach so ugly."

Ma delivered me at 1:23 a.m. under the sign of the Ox. Ma said: "What's an ox usually doing at one o'clock in the morning? Sleeping, right?" Toronto is twelve hours behind Hong Kong. Had I been born in Hong Kong, it would have been the middle of the day, when an ox is expected to be hard at work in the fields. Ma took this opportunity to credit herself, again, for giving me an easy life, as if she had always planned my nocturnal birth.

During this time, the rest of Dad's family started settling in Canada. His parents were among the last to arrive. They came shortly after I was born. Ma recalls that there was a family summit to decide where my grandparents would live.

Everyone had an excuse about why it wasn't convenient for them to take in my grandparents until they were able to secure permanent residency. In the end, the responsibility fell to my parents, and they moved out of their cozy apartment and bought a bigger house to accommodate the older generation. Filial Piety was at work once again. Ma believed it was their duty to take them in.

So Ma went back to work when I was just a few months old. By then, she was working full-time at a hardware store and then driving downtown to wait tables at a hotel. She'd leave me with Dad's parents and return home well after I'd been put to bed. The new house was an ambitious purchase. Dad had to put off his studies to make enough hours in the accounting department of a computer company so that they could keep up with the mortgage payments. He was frustrated that his life plans were constantly being rerouted because of the demands of his family. Ma was the one, between them, who rationalized their decisions, who refused to indulge in bitterness and instead kept them focused. She found herself in a familiar position. Just as when she was a young girl, she was looking after everyone else and feeling unappreciated.

And it turns out she was an easy target. The Squawking Chicken was the Squawking Chicken: loud, outspoken, honest. She was not like the other Lui wives and daughters, relegated to the corners of the room while the men stayed in the center. The Squawking Chicken belonged in the center too. But the Luis were intimidated by Ma's behavior and style of communication. Ma came to realize, too late, that they lacked confidence and were therefore threatened by hers. They misinterpreted her volume for arrogance. Their insecurities prevented them from seeing that Ma was always well intentioned. It's just that they couldn't get past the voice . . . and the nails.

One night Ma was summoned into her living room after she'd come home from work, tired and hungry, to answer to charges from my uncle. My grandparents were upset that they were being forced to babysit me, and Ma's attitude wasn't grateful enough. She was ordered to kneel and apologize. In her own home, a home she struggled to pay for, a home that she bought so that her in-laws could be comfortable, even though it meant taking time away from me, her only child. At first, Ma refused. But she had no support. Because Dad could not act. Shamed by what he believed were his own inadequacies, and unable to overcome his insecurity and weakness—the same characteristics he shared with his kin—he was, then, a man incapable of defending his wife. He stayed in the basement, smoking, hating himself

but paralyzed by fear. Without an ally, without anyone to have her back, the Squawking Chicken had no choice but to drop to her knees. Dad's inaction rendered Ma powerless. For the second time in her life, she'd been betrayed by family.

My parents' marriage deteriorated after that. For the next six years, the Squawking Chicken was silenced. Until one night, after a brutal fight with Dad, she realized it was time to set herself on fire again. The phoenix was molting. She had given his family everything and there was nothing left. Not even me. She was bitter and desperately unhappy, to the point where her health had started to decline. She had no savings. She had no prospects. There was no way she could take me with her. She felt she had no choice but to go back to Hong Kong, alone, without me, not wanting to disrupt my life or compromise the better opportunities I would have in Canada. It was a heartbreaking, excruciating decision, not only because she had to let go of me temporarily, but also because, after all that had happened, she was still in love with Dad. But the situation had become impossible. On the day of her departure, she told Dad two things: "I will fuck you up if you fuck up our daughter." And "I will come back to you if you make something of yourself."

And then she was gone.

While Dad and I were adjusting to our lives without her, Ma was rebuilding hers in Hong Kong. She started dating my stepfather the following year after she and Dad had officially divorced. He was kind and generous and he promised her that he would provide for me too. After years of struggle, after being put down by my father's family, after shouldering her own family's scandals, she was finally allowed to be comfortable. She sent for me as soon as she had settled. It was decided that I would live in Canada with Dad during the school year but that I would spend all holidays with Ma and my stepfather in Hong Kong—two weeks at Christmas, two weeks during spring break and the entire summer. My stepfather was indeed as kind and generous to me as he was to her. He kept his promise.

"What do you think of your accusations now?" Ma asked me when she finished her story. "If you want to say I fucked off with another man, who do you think I was doing it for?"

Sitting across from her that day in the coffee shop, after listening to Ma confide to me the rationale behind her decisions, and the sacrifices that had preceded them, I finally understood that she left me *for* me. That in doing so, my father became more responsible because he was now responsible for me. That having to raise me by himself was the motivation he needed to make something of himself, and he did. I also understood that in the end, she was proud of Dad and of what he had accomplished.

"I regret nothing," Ma concluded. Because in doing what she did, I was better for it.

Then she finished her coffee and went off to find the rest of our group in the mall, leaving me to think about what I had just learned. It was a pretty theatrical exit. She wears her watch loose on her wrist so she's always shaking it so that it'll fall back into place. She shook it extra vigorously this time when she got up out of her seat, stretching her fingers out wide so that her hands seemed even longer with the added length of those long red nails. Then she tossed her hair back and walked deliberately out of the shop. Very Old Hollywood. Looking back, it was like a performance she'd been rehearsing for a long time. At that moment, though, I felt bad. I knew I had fucked up. But at the same time, I also felt like I had just met my ma for the first time. And it was the first time I felt the surge of real, mature love—not the cuddly kind of love you have for the mommy who takes care of your basic food and water needs, but the profound kind of love for the mother who shows you how to be a real person. This love is an exclusive understanding between two people who have always been connected, who will always be connected. I didn't know consciously then, but I can tell you now that that was the seed of awareness: that my relationship with my ma will be the greatest, most important relationship I will ever have in my life. And I wanted to thank her for it.

Using the money I had originally intended to spend on that dress, I went instead to the jewelry store. I could only afford gold hoops. Gold because it was her favorite. Then I went to find her. She was waiting by the mall exit with the rest of our group. I presented them to her in front of them. I apologized for my behavior and told her that to make up for my poor attitude and the horrible accusations I wanted her to have the earrings. She picked them out of my hands, those red nails slowly, ceremoniously separating the clasp, attaching them to each earlobe.

"Do you like them?" I asked her.

"Do *you* like them?" she asked me back.

I said I did. And she said, "Good. It doesn't matter if I like them. But it matters that you like them. It matters that you like and remember the times that you thank me. You will be thanking me for your entire life."

∂⑥

My husband, Jacek, and I have decided not to have children. It wasn't always this way. Even after we got married, we always assumed it would happen. Mostly because that's just what people do. And then I was asked to babysit my brother-in-law's three children, two boys and a girl, who were then five, three and just under a year old. It was a devastating afternoon. There were bathroom accidents. They were so full of need, unrelenting need. I was exhausted when I came home. And it was only three hours! So we started asking ourselves—do we really want to be parents? Did I really want to be a mother?

And I came to accept that I don't for all the "superficial" reasons—the time, the sacrifice, my career, the desire to travel without having to worry about dependents, the freedom to sleep in, to spend my money on myself. And I'm now at the age when even if I were to change my mind, and I haven't, I couldn't do anything about it.

I have no doubts about this. Neither does Ma. The Squawking Chicken has never pressured for grandchildren. She doesn't want them. Specifically she doesn't want them because she doesn't want to be asked to take care of them.

I, then, will never reap the rewards of Filial Piety. I will never have a child who is obligated to pay me back. I will never have a daughter who says one day that our relationship is the greatest, most important relationship of her life. I will never have a child who will be responsible for my happiness, or whose happiness is predicated upon mine. Because Filial

Piety worked on me. Because my mother's happiness is the greatest happiness of my life. And if she was selfish in achieving it, what it taught me was selflessness. What makes me happiest is that my happiness is not singular. It is not my own. I share it with her. I owe it to her. It belongs to her. And that is enough.

CHAPTER 5

I Should Have Given Birth to a Piece of Barbecue Pork

Ma knew from the very beginning that I was a child who would require a controlling and firm hand. My father's monk master told her so. Dad's monk master, Sifu, was a true Buddhist monk. He lived in poverty and prayed at a run-down temple just outside Dad's home village. When Dad was thirteen, he used to pass him every day on the way to school. Unlike the other boys, Dad was never mean to the monk. Dad wouldn't make fun of him for being dirty. He wouldn't make a big production out of stepping away from the monk on the street.

The first time they talked, it was pouring rain and Dad's clothes were soaked as he walked home. The monk invited him to take shelter for a while in his shabby hut. My father has always been an introvert. He was the quiet, studious one among his nine brothers and sisters. Dad enjoyed the tranquility he experienced in the monk's presence. He appreciated that the monk was at peace with quietness and solitude. So he began stopping by the monk's every day after school. Their conversations were spare. Instead, they connected through silence. Later on, the monk explained to Dad that comfort in silence is a fundamental Buddhist principle on the path to enlightenment. The monk became dad's Buddhist mentor and, as I've mentioned before, Dad seriously considered becoming a monk himself before he met Ma. She ended up redirecting him, but Dad was still very devoted to his monk master and always consulted him, when possible, on important matters. Ma respected Dad's relationship with Sifu. It set him apart from many of the other young men of his generation, whom she described as "fah-fah feet-feet," too slick, too smooth, all playboys. Dad was totally not a playboy. He would rather hang out in Sifu's shack than at the bar. One of my parents' great regrets about moving to Canada was that they were no longer in regular contact with Sifu.

I was only a few months old when my parents brought me back to Hong Kong for the first time. Dad wanted to present me to Sifu for a blessing. Sifu took me, all bundled up in blankets, in his arms. Ma remembers that he and I were very still together. I had stopped fussing as soon as he put his hand on my head. He stayed like that for a while and then asked Dad to fetch him some ink and scroll paper. Sifu wrote out four words:

Yeem Gah Goon Gao
(Strict Family Control Teach)

We don't use connecting words in Chinese like "to" or "by" or "at." The traditional written language is spare, nouns and verbs only, but the meaning is made clear by how the words are ordered. *Yeem gah goon gao* means that proper instruction comes from discipline and control. Sifu was telling my parents that they would need to be strict with me. That I would require close and constant governance to stay on course.

Ma took Sifu's counsel very seriously. If she ever doubted her parenting tactics, if she ever worried that she was too harsh, she would pull out Sifu's scroll and it would strengthen her resolve. She would be strict with me to keep me on course. And she would do this by shaming me.

The first time Ma publicly shamed me I was nine years old. It was an ordinary summer evening, and we were at my grandmother's mah-jong den in Hong Kong. After dim sum (around lunchtime) three or four times a week, Ma and I would head over to Grandmother's for a game. I spent hours there watching and memorizing Ma's mannerisms—her long red nails rearranging and stacking tiles, doing it all with one hand if she was smoking—and watching and memorizing Chinese kung fu soap operas. The soap operas were serialized, broadcast in prime time every night, Monday to Friday. That year, I was obsessed with *The Legend of the Condor Heroes*. I was a total fangirl.

The female lead in *The Legend of the Condor Heroes* was an actress named Barbara Yung Mei Ling who played the iconic Wong Yung character. The television series was based on a popular book series set during the Song Dynasty in China about the adventures of a young couple, Wong Yung and Guo Jing. Wong Yung was different from the girls typically depicted in Chinese folklore. For starters, she was brilliant, one of the most brilliant minds in all of Chinese literature. She outsmarted the boys all the time. And she had an attitude. She talked back. She wouldn't take shit from anybody. And, obviously, she was really pretty. She wore the best traditional robes. And her hair was awesome, always in pretty braids arranged in complicated loops and tails that fell adorably around her face. She had an expressive face, as played by Barbara Yung. Yung had dancing, mischievous eyes and a precocious smile, features that she used to great effect in taking on the role. She had two prominent front teeth that were slightly crooked, giving her mouth an overbite effect that only added to her appeal. Barbara was the most famous actress in Hong Kong at the time. Even Ma found her irresistible. She would always say that Barbara Yung is very *sahng mahng*. It's an expression used to describe someone who is very active, who never stops. *Sahng* literally means "alive." And *mahng* means "strong." Barbara Yung was alive and strong. Or so we thought.

After every episode of *The Legend of the Condor Heroes*, I would pretend to be Wong Yung, reenacting the plot and imitating her moves. That night, Wong Yung had been made temporary leader of the Beggars' Tribe. Her master, Old Beggar Hong, the proper leader of the Beggars' Tribe, had been poisoned and had gone into exile for several months so that he could heal in time for the Mount Wah kung fu tournament. The tournament was the pinnacle of the *Legend of the Condor Heroes* story line. The victor of the tournament was declared the greatest kung fu artist of the time. Wong Yung's master was considered one of the four favorites to win. Before leaving for rehabilitation so that he could compete at full strength, Old Beggar Hong declared that Wong Yung would be the boss of his tribe during his absence. The only problem was that his Fighting Jade Stick, his signature weapon, had been stolen by the dastardly Yeung Kuo. Wong Yung was charged with mobilizing the Beggars' Tribe

against Yeung and retrieving the Jade Stick. To prove that she was a true pupil of Old Beggar Hong and the rightful heir of the Fighting Jade Stick, though, Wong had to demonstrate that she knew how to use it. The martial arts specialty that accompanied the Fighting Jade Stick was called the Dog Fighting Technique, a series of moves that made its opponents look like a pack of sorry dogs.

My Fighting Jade Stick was a ruler. I used it to fight imaginary dogs all around my grandmother's living room, cramped with three tables of mah-jong players, four people to a table. I slashed my Jade Stick ruler through the air, hitting my imaginary adversary in the head before drop-kicking him to the ground. I turned quickly to intercept an incoming punch to the back of my neck, blocking it with my ruler in one hand and using the other hand to slap the insurgent twice across the face. Wong Yung had just done this on television with great panache. Then I swiveled to my right, lunging forward with the elegance of a gymnast, striking the next opponent in the throat, precisely hitting his Adam's apple . . . which happened to be Ma's thigh. She was just then picking up her next tile, which also happened to be the winning tile. And since I'd just jabbed her leg like a dog with the Fighting Jade Stick, the tile fell out of her hand, tumbling off the mah-jong board, scattering the blocks all over the floor, defaulting the entire hand and resulting in her losing a huge pot.

Oh. Fuck.

There was no time to run. And I couldn't have run even if there was. The Squawking Chicken's eyes had kung fu powers of their own. They were capable of paralyzing their targets. They widened and narrowed at the same time, growing bigger from top to bottom, and stretching from side to side, a geometry-bending Chinese double Cyclops. It was terrifying. And that was only the prelude to the squawk. In my entire adult life I have never been as scared shitless as I was in that moment. Not bungee-jumping, not public speaking, not driving at 200 mph on a NASCAR racetrack—

never have I been so afraid as I was the night I stabbed the Squawking Chicken with a ruler during a mah-jong game.

So there I was, holding my Fighting Jade Stick that had turned back into a flimsy ruler, shrinking as my mother fixed her eyes on me, knowing that I'd just cost her a win. And that's when she said it, a pronouncement she'd repeat throughout my childhood whenever I disappointed her: "I should have given birth to a piece of barbecue pork. It doesn't last but at least it tastes good and doesn't make trouble. Why did I give birth to something that only gives me trouble?!" I was embarrassed and ashamed. She basically told an entire room of mah-jong ladies that I was worth less than a piece of barbecue pork.

That wasn't the only time Ma shamed me because of Barbara Yung. I had started wearing a retainer a couple of years after the ruler incident. My top two front teeth weren't in line with the rest, and they were a little crooked . . . kinda like Barbara Yung's. Barbara Yung was still my idol, even after *The Legend of the Condor Heroes* had concluded. But on May 14, 1985, Barbara Yung committed suicide. The newspapers reported she was heartbroken over her boyfriend and, amid rumors that he may have been seeing someone else, left the gas on in her apartment, dying of carbon monoxide poisoning.

Barbara was twenty-six years old, at the height of her

fame. Hong Kong was practically shut down for her funeral. I was eleven, and I watched the news coverage in Canada on television. I made my dad buy every memorial magazine that was available at the Chinese supermarket. I wore Chinese traditional robes to school. I was despondent. So I decided to honor Barbara with my teeth. We would be teeth twins forever. It was how I would remember her: I threw out my retainer. Dumped it in the trash, not telling Dad about it until after the garbage had been collected.

Dad was furious. That retainer was expensive. And it was anathema to the immigrant mentality—to toss out something perfectly functional . . . for sentiment! But he didn't punish me. Instead, he decided that I should be the one to tell Ma when I visited her in Hong Kong a month later for my school holidays. That year, I begged Dad not to send me to Hong Kong, knowing I'd be in deep shit with Ma about the retainer. Dad ignored me. I was sullen and bratty on the way to the airport. I gave him a really pissy hug before passing through the gates. When I looked back he was grinning.

Ma was there, as usual, waiting for me in the arrivals area of Hong Kong's Kai Tak airport. As always, I noticed her right away. It's not like you could miss her. As soon as she saw me she started squawking, both to get my attention and to draw attention to herself. She seemed like she was in a good mood. I thought I might be able to get away with not mentioning my retainer immediately. Turns out that wasn't an option. She asked me about it immediately.

"Why are your teeth still crooked? Where's your retainer?"

I had no choice but to tell her. As briefly as possible, I told her that it ended up in the trash, like almost by accident. Ma wanted the details. So then I tried to play it off like it was uncomfortable and/or it wasn't working anymore. The more I dodged, the worse I made it for myself. Ma is suspicious by default. She could always smell when I wasn't being honest.

"You don't have to tell me the truth. But this is your opportunity to tell me the way you want to tell me."

Ma never had to elaborate on the "or else" part. It all came out then. My mourning over Barbara Yung. My desire to cement her memory with my teeth. My obsession to *be* Barbara, if only in the mouth. At the end of my confession, I became defiant. I told Ma that these were *my* teeth. It was *my* mouth. It was *my* face. I could do whatever I wanted. That she couldn't make me get another retainer. I refused.

Ma's reaction: "Fine. You're the one who has to live with it." And then she laughed and laughed and laughed. She laughed all the way home from the airport. She could not stop laughing. Her laughing only made me angrier. And more afraid.

After dropping my bags off and tidying up, we went out to meet Ma's family for dinner. Grandmother and Grandfather were there, as well as my aunts and uncles and their husbands and wives. Also some of my younger cousins. Ma waited until the first course was served.

"Do you all notice something special about Elaine's teeth? Everyone, look at Elaine's teeth. Elaine, show Grandmother your teeth. Can you see her teeth? Do you know why her teeth are like that? Elaine, tell them about your teeth."

She told them about my teeth. She told them about my expensive retainer sacrificed in memory of Barbara Yung. She told them about how I was preserving Barbara Yung's memory. She told them that Barbara Yung was my tooth idol. She was loud and detailed and repetitive. By the end of the story, everyone else was laughing too.

It was the same the next day, when we met my Uncle and Auntie Lai for dim sum. Auntie Lai is my godmother. She and her husband have three children and her youngest son, Peter, is my ma's godson. Peter is a year older than me. His sister, Sandra, is four years older than him. And their eldest brother, Thomas, my first crush, is a year older than her. I was always the baby of the group. Peter always made fun of me to impress his siblings, and I was always trying to impress all of them. So I was mortified when Ma started in on the story about my retainer. I begged her to stop. And, of course, she wouldn't. She reminded me of my own words. Those are *your* teeth. *Your* mouth. *Your* face. *Your* life. Don't you want to stand up for Barbara Yung's life? All summer long, she told the story of my retainer. Every time there was a new audience, my Barbara Yung teeth and my discarded retainer became the topic of conversation.

The thing is, my dental dedication to Barbara Yung's memory sounded so much more noble in my own head than it did when I heard Ma explaining it to people over and over and over again. In fact, it sounded really stupid. What kind of an idiot fucks with her own teeth over a dead actress? The Squawking Chicken's voice stripped away all the glamour and drama I'd attached to my retainer decision. It exposed the foolishness of my actions. In making me listen to the story, repeatedly, she broke down the juvenile romanticism that compelled me to throw out that retainer, and all the subsequent rationalizations I had built up inside myself to justify what I'd done. And it was that much more effective because she had an audience. The audience wasn't for her. The audience was for me. The audience ensured that the story, her telling of it, landed with me each and every time, knowing that I'd know that there were fresh ears to hear it, and to judge it for what it was—totally moronic.

There was a second benefit to the Squawking Chicken's public shaming of me for my retainer. At the end of the summer, before she sent me home, I asked her if she was going to make me get a new one. She told me that she and Dad had discussed it over the phone and that they had agreed that they wouldn't be taking me back to the dentist to refit me for another. This was partly due to finances. But my teeth were *almost* straight anyway. More importantly, though, Ma said that I would have to learn to live with the consequence. She cautioned that a couple of crooked teeth was getting off easy. It wasn't permanently damaging. It wouldn't alter the course of my life. But that it was a good, lasting reminder, every time I opened my mouth, of a rash, ill-conceived decision I had made in my youth. Then she explained the motivation for why she kept at me about the retainer, all summer long, every chance she got, and always in front of other people. Ma was preparing me for future criticism: "My criticism of you always comes from a place of love. But as you get older, your critics won't love you. They will criticize you to hurt you. I am preparing you for criticism that comes from your enemies."

By verbally assaulting me all summer, by shaming me publicly, by constantly reminding me of my mistake, the Squawking Chicken was not only teaching me how to live with it, but inuring me to the criticism that would result from it. She wanted me to learn how to take it. She was helping me figure out how to deal with it. She was showing me how to recognize when to eat it when I was wrong, how to grow from it and move forward, and, when I was ready, how to use it to get stronger.

This was also the reason she shamed me by comparing me unfavorably to a piece of barbecue pork when I struck her in the leg with my Fighting Jade Stick ruler. The immediate lesson, of course, was that children shouldn't run around irresponsibly with rulers flying around in the air. People get hurt. How many times have you seen kids these days playing with something they probably shouldn't be and one of them ending up in tears? The parents rationalize and apologize in hushed tones. The ruler-wielding culprit is reasoned with, and five minutes later he's doing it again.

Me? The Fighting Jade Stick was never again seen at my grandmother's mah-jong den. I spent the rest of that evening at my mother's feet, singing the theme song to *The Legend of the Condor Heroes*, not knocking over any other tiles; I was rewarded for being obedient at the end of the night with a "bonus chip" from every mah-jong lady at the table.

As you can imagine, though, if this had gone down in present-day North America at a yummy mummy play group, they'd probably call child services on Ma's ass for abuse. Shame isn't considered an effective parenting device these days. But shame was one of the Squawking Chicken's most effective parenting devices. Because there is nothing like the impression left behind by shame. People remember their shame. Children remember their shame. And if the shame resulted from a mistake they made, well, there's a really good chance they won't make that mistake again. That's what my ma believed. In her mind, shame is one of the consequences of doing something wrong. And it is perhaps the *least* consequential consequence of doing something wrong. As she explained it to me later that night—*You are lucky that you only hurt me tonight and that you didn't seriously injure someone else. If you hurt someone else, you would owe that person for life. You would be saying sorry for life. You would be under that person forever. You are lucky Mama only embarrassed you. Mama embarrassing you is much better than you having to say sorry to Mrs. Tam forever. You would be indebted to Mrs. Tam forever. No daughter of mine will ever have to say sorry to that Mrs. Tam.* (Therein followed a story about how Mrs. Tam always cheated.) *Better to be shamed and disciplined by someone who loves you, who will never use your mistakes against you, than to send you off into the world unprepared, to be shamed by outsiders who will never forgive and never forget.*

Ma definitely never forgot Scarecrow Chiu's son. Scarecrow Chiu (a nickname Ma gave her because she was so thin) was one of Ma's regular mah-jong mates in our gated community, Fairview Park, in Hong Kong. I was twelve, the year after my retainer drama, when Ma and my stepfather bought a house in the new development. It was set up like a Stepford community—cookie-cutter Western-style homes with drives on numbered streets in lettered blocks. We lived on 4th Street in J Block, number 35. My godparents had moved there the year before. When Ma went to visit, she fell in love with the neighborhood because it reminded her of the Canadian subdivision we'd once lived in. She wanted me to be able to hop on my bike and ride around safely when I came to see her every summer. I was getting older and she knew I'd be bored just hanging out with her at mah-jong all day. There was a country club at Fairview Park. Ma became a member and I'd go swimming there with the other mah-jong orphans every afternoon while our mothers gambled from day into night. After dinner, the mothers would resume their games and we'd take our bikes down to the ravine, eat ice cream, listen to music, play card games, and flirt with the other Fairview Park kids. It was innocent adolescent mischief. But there was one kid who took it to another level.

Scarecrow Chiu's youngest son, Little Geet, was a sweet kid. He wasn't mean-spirited, but he had a wild streak and way too much energy, even for us, and we were all scamps. When the rest of us went home, Geet would set off firecrackers near the convenience store all by himself. He got busted for stealing fish balls at the noodle stalls. He was constantly punking the security guards who manned the booth at the Fairview Park main entrance, buzzing the alarms for no reason, or jamming the gates so that cars couldn't get through. Pretty soon he had a reputation around the neighborhood. And every time he screwed up, his mother, Scarecrow Chiu, would make excuses for him.

One night, the mothers decided to have dinner at the country club. We kids had spent the afternoon at the pool and we were told to meet our parents in the dining room after getting changed. Ma asked me where Little Geet was when I sat down at the table. I told her we hadn't seen him all day. Scarecrow Chiu called home, he wasn't there. She called park security. They said they hadn't seen him either. Everyone started to worry. By now he was an hour late for dinner. One of the mah-jong aunties was married to a cop. She was about to tell him to put out a search when Geet walked into the dining room, on top of the world. Turns out he'd snuck out to go into town with some of his older friends from school to play video games. If that had been me, my ma would have skinned me, right there in front of the entire country club membership, with no hesitation. So I thought, well shit, Little Geet is going to get it.

But Scarecrow Chiu just told her son how worried she'd

been about him and to never do that again. Then she asked the kitchen staff to warm up some food because he was hungry. The Squawking Chicken was unimpressed. She was so unimpressed that she tried to shame Little Geet on Scarecrow Chiu's behalf. She laid into him for stressing out his mother. She lectured him for being irresponsible, and for potentially putting himself in danger by not telling anyone where he was going. She spent the whole rest of the dinner itemizing his mistakes until his head hung low, and he pushed away his plate, no longer in the mood to eat. Which is when Scarecrow Chiu pleaded with Ma to stop, defending Little Geet, blaming herself for not providing enough activities to keep him occupied during the day. Ma wasn't having it. She then announced to the rest of us that because of Little Geet's adventure, we were now all expected to *boe doe*, or check in, every ninety minutes, no matter what, no matter where we were. Fairview Park, back then, was small enough anyway so that you could get from one end to the other in ten minutes on a bike. Ma decided that ten minutes out of every couple of hours wouldn't stop our fun. Reluctantly, we agreed. That was the beginning of what would become my lifelong habit of *boe doe*-ing. Even now, whatever I'm doing, wherever I am, I check in with my mother. When I get into a cab, I call her. When the cab drops me off, I call her. When I'm out with the dogs, I call her. At the end of the walk, I call her. I *boe doe* all the time. I just never want Ma to have to wonder where I am. I want her to be able to picture me. The world feels whole when we know where the other is.

That night, none of us dared to ask to go back out. Except, of course, for Little Geet. As soon as dinner was over, he begged his ma to let him go play basketball. She eventually agreed. While we were all walking back to our houses, I listened as Ma pleaded with Scarecrow Chiu to put some limits on her son's behavior. Little Geet has a kind, gentle heart, Ma said, but he needs direction and he's too easily swayed. Scarecrow kept insisting that it was fine, that he was a good boy who just needed his space. But Ma warned Scarecrow that if she didn't rein him in now, she would regret it. That she was doing him a disservice by not only not giving him structure, but also by not calling him out on his mistakes, by sparing him of guilt, by sparing him of shame and humiliation when he was wrong. Because he never thought twice before he fucked up, she was setting him up for failure in the long run. Scarecrow stayed silent. She wasn't strong enough to discipline her child.

The Squawking Chicken ended up being right. A few weeks later, Little Geet, who was underage, took his parents' car out for a joyride. He lost control and smashed it into the playground. At dim sum the next day, Scarecrow dismissed the incident, saying that insurance would cover it and that all boys are fascinated by cars anyway, and that Little Geet had learned his lesson. I wasn't allowed to hang out with Little Geet anymore after that. When I returned to Hong Kong the following summer, Ma told me that Little Geet had started running drugs for the triads. Gradually, as Little Geet's criminal involvement increased, Scarecrow pulled back from the mah-jong group, embarrassed by her son's shady activities. Ma and her friends tried to reach out to her but by then she couldn't face people anymore, blaming her own weakness for Little Geet's fate. Little Geet died when he was twenty-two of a heroin overdose. Scarecrow was the one who found him in the bathtub. I was in college when Ma called to tell me. She was very, very sad when she found out.

Ma had seen firsthand the devastating effects that drugs could have on a family. Her greatest fear was that I would try drugs and screw up my life. Two of her five siblings were drug addicts. Many of her childhood friends in Yuen Long became drug addicts. Their lives were wasted, just like Little Geet's. There was no way her daughter would ever use. We'd be at the Fairview Park country club and she'd bring it up, out of the blue, over dessert if someone happened to compliment me. *Wah, Elaine is getting so tall. What lovely skin.*

"It won't be lovely if she ever does drugs. She'll be like my sister who had druggie pockmarks all over her face."

We'd be over at Uncle and Auntie Lai's for dinner and their perfect, pretty, smart daughter Sandra would bring home a volleyball trophy and Ma would point to Sandra and then to me and say, apropos of nothing, "If you ever do drugs, you'll never be like Sandra, you'll be a total loser with a gross body and nobody will want to come near your disgusting hands. Drug addicts always have ugly hands."

This is what I call the Squawking Chicken's famous Pre-Shame. Ma was constantly pre-shaming me, humiliating me in advance, making me afraid of the shame so that I'd never be foolish enough to earn it. Ma used Pre-Shame to scare me away from drugs. She relentlessly beat it into my head that drugs would be my downfall. Pre-Shame was kinda like Ma's version of Pavlovian conditioning—protecting me from doing whatever it was that she didn't want me to do by giving me a taste of what I could expect if I ever did it. By the time I was old enough to be exposed to the drug culture, I was totally resistant.

While shame was used to build up my immunity to drug temptation, Ma also used shame to build my confidence, and in particular my body confidence. Women struggle with their physical self-perception all the time. We want to be thinner, curvier, taller, shorter, fuller breasted, more ample assed, it never stops. But I've never met a woman who is as satisfied with her physical appearance as the Squawking Chicken. With the exception of when she's been ill, Ma has always admired her own body. When she was fit, she flaunted it. If she gains weight, she celebrates it. She'll be on the couch, with her stomach gathering over her pants, and she'll grab a handful of fleshy rolls, chortling, and talk about how what's growing on her belly is keeping her skin smooth. "Old woman no good too thin," she'll say to my husband.

And when he replies, "Ma, you look good!" her response reliably will always be: "I am always look good!"

Perhaps it's that she had to reclaim her own body after her rape. Perhaps it's having been through so many health crises that she appreciates the parts of her that are actually working. Whatever it is, it's not bravado. She genuinely believes that she always looks good. But she saw early on that as a young girl I was insecure about my appearance. Growing up a Chinese girl in North America, surrounded by blondes and brunettes, with blue and green and gray eyes, long, straight noses, and versatile wavy and curly hair, I longed not to be "other." I hated that I was. I was ashamed of my appearance. I was ashamed of my body. So Ma shamed me to stop me from shaming myself. It seems counterintuitive and it's

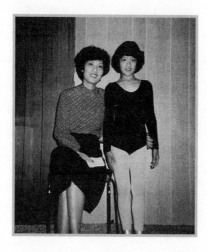

certainly not consistent with the nurturing, supportive techniques child psychologists in North America might recommend to parents hoping to build their kids' self-esteem. But there's a saying in Chinese that goes *Yee duk gung duk*— "Use poison fight poison," the Chinese equivalent of "fight fire with fire." Ma fought my body shame by shaming me, publicly.

What could be more mortifying than bra shopping for the first time? I was ten. My body was being weird. My breasts were growing and I started becoming conscious of my nipples showing through my T-shirts. Jennifer, the blond girl who lived across the street, a year older, had already started wearing a bra and loved showing off her bra strap. I decided to wait until summer to get a bra because I didn't want to introduce one into my life in the middle of the school year. My parents were living apart then and I was staying with my father. Ma was in Hong Kong and I went to see her for the summer holiday. As soon as I met her in the arrivals area at the airport she was all over me about not standing up straight. I told her I needed a bra and that I didn't want people to see my body. She told me that if people had a problem with my body, it was their issue and not mine. The next day she took me to the department store.

Right away, Ma went over to the saleslady and started asking about training bras. I slowly moved away to hide in the far corner of the intimates section, trying to figure out how I could strangle myself with panty hose. All of a sudden, it was like an announcement coming over the PA system, only not. Just Ma, with that goddamn voice, calling me over. And in English, because Ma liked to show off in Hong Kong that she had a daughter who spoke English.

"ELAINE, I FOUND ANUDDA BLAH FOR YOUUUUUUUUUUUUU!"

Every head turned. Every shopper on that floor knew that I needed a bra. I was the girl with the situation coming out of her chest that had to be taken care of. I rushed over to Ma, took her hand, and pulled her into the dressing room, begging her to be quiet, pleading with her not to publicize my junior breasts and bra requirements. She was so angry at my reaction, she spat out the following lecture, in English, just to make sure I would understand her in the language I used in my mind: "Your body, this natural. What you need, bra, this natural. Why you shame for something natural? Why you shame your body? If you shame your body, you shame yourself. When you shame yourself, everyone shame you."

Ma was urging me to confront my own body and its changes to confront the truth about puberty. Over and over again, through my adolescence, she used shame to help me accept the reality of what I looked like, to *see* what I actually looked like so that I would stop trying to look like something else.

The summer after Grade 8 I returned to Hong Kong for summer holiday with copper hair. I'd been spraying it with a product that lightens hair when you apply heat to it. It's supposed to make you blond. Since my hair is naturally black, the closest I could come was orange. Still, I did it so that whenever people would ask me about it, I'd lie and say that one of my parents was white. Ma shamed me for weeks like she did with my Barbara Yung teeth and the retainer.

She kept calling it "red hooker head" because the prostitutes who worked in the clubs always dyed their hair. Everywhere we went: "Do you know why Elaine has a red hooker head? Because she thinks she's a *gwai mui* [white girl]! I spent a night with Alain Delon and she's our secret love child!" And they all laughed.

Looking back, of course it was humiliating. Ma's relentless shaming was difficult to endure. But she wasn't shaming me for sport. It's not like it was a good time for her either. As a Chinese girl growing up in North America, I was struggling with my cultural identity. As a first-generation child born to immigrants, there was no model for me to follow; I was part of a new breed. And the Squawking Chicken was the only Chinese force in my life who could help me find the balance between my environment and my heritage. Ma shamed me so that I would not suppress the Chinese part of myself to try to become something I could never be. I would never be a North American white girl. But I could be a North American girl with a Chinese background. I could stop being ashamed of being a North American girl with a Chinese background.

It took a lot of work. The North American influence can be overpowering. Through my teen years, surrounded by white friends, the Chinese half of me was like wax, soft and malleable against the heat of desire to blend in. And every time I wanted contact lenses to lighten my eyes or picked the wrong shade of foundation to lighten my skin, Ma was there. To shame me—yes. But really to remind me who I was, to rebuild me.

CHAPTER 6

Miss Hong Kong Is a Whore

J don't ever remember Ma telling me that I was beautiful.
It's not that she ever said I was ugly. Or that she didn't, on
occasion, tell me I looked nice, even pretty. But between Ma
and me, there's never been that mother-daughter movie moment, somewhere in the third act, when she's held my hand
and through eyes brimming with tears, she's whispered, her
voice choked with emotion: *"Baby, you are so beautiful."*

For *starters, Ma and I don't speak like that to each other.*
Actually, we don't speak like that to anyone. Ma abhors affection—
physical and verbal. She's not great with hugs—giving or
receiving. And corny talk is gross to her. This is partly cultural. "I love you" in Chinese is super, super cringey. In our
language, people just don't say it like that, straight up. We
might say, "I care about you a lot." Or "I like you so much,"

but actually uttering those three words, "I love you," is uncommon. It sounds weird. It sounds uncomfortably intimate. "I love you" is used only between lovers, never as a general expression of feeling between anyone in any other kind of relationship, and even then it's reserved for those very rare occasions, in total privacy and never as an open declaration.

But the Squawking Chicken's emotional reticence goes beyond the standard Chinese reserve. She's just not one to share her affection through words or gestures. Ma prefers to show her love through action. So if she ever did tell me she loves me, or that I'm beautiful, I think I would laugh. Or rush her to the hospital. Because that would be a sign that she'd gone insane. These are just not words that would ever come out of Ma's mouth. Quite the opposite, in fact.

I was eleven years old when Ma first told me I wasn't beautiful. Of course, we were at Grandmother's mah-jong den. While Ma played, I watched the Miss Hong Kong pageant on TV. Back then, the Miss Hong Kong pageant was a big deal. There were only two main broadcasters in Hong Kong in the eighties. TVB was the most watched and most powerful. It had the resources to turn Miss Hong Kong into the major event of the summer, splitting each round into a weekend special, so that the pageant took up almost an entire month. *Everyone* watched Miss Hong Kong. *Everyone* talked about Miss Hong Kong. And *every* little girl wanted to be Miss Hong Kong.

It was the day of the semifinals. The favorite that year was Joyce Godenzi, born to an Australian father and Chinese mother. Godenzi was gorgeous, with wide-set eyes and curly hair, a totally different aesthetic than all the other contestants. Hong Kong was obsessed with her. I was obsessed with her. I practiced walking like her. I threw a shawl around my shoulders, pretending it was the Miss Hong Kong cape that's presented to the winner when she's crowned. I clutched a soup ladle in both hands, imagining it was the diamond scepter that Miss Hong Kong carried around on her victory lap. I worked on my smile in the mirror, hoping to achieve a combination of sweetness and whatever my idea of intrigue was at the time.

My biggest concern in previous years had been the question-and-answer section. I worried that my Chinese answers wouldn't be good enough, since English was my first language and I couldn't read or write in Chinese. But Joyce took care of that. Joyce's Chinese wasn't great either, and all the aunties talked about how this was an advantage because being a foreign-raised candidate was considered exotic.

That afternoon, Ma's sister was on her way to get her hair done. Ma wanted me out of the way for a while so she told me to tag along. One of the other stylists at the salon had extra time and ended up curling my hair into ringlets, just like Joyce Godenzi (sort of). When we returned to Grandmother's, all the mah-jong aunties, and Grandmother too, went bananas over how pretty I looked. They said I was so pretty, I could enter the Miss Hong Kong pageant in a few years. This made my life . . . for about thirty seconds. Until the Squawking Chicken weighed in: "You're not pretty enough to be Miss Hong Kong. *I* could have been Miss Hong Kong. But Miss Hong Kong is a whore."

It's true. Ma was a first-class beauty. I've seen the photos—because she shows them to me all the time. While I do resemble her, I'm also half my father, and she reminds me of this all the time too. "It's too bad you got your stocky body and thick legs from your dad's side."

All the aunties reacted like you're probably reacting right now. How could she say that to a little girl? Let her dream. But for Ma, dreaming was the problem. "Dream? Stop putting dreams in her head. You think I bust my ass raising a daughter just so she could be a beauty pageant whore?"

Most people in Hong Kong believe that the Hong Kong entertainment system is corrupt. And many people believed that Miss Hong Kongs were just glorified escorts for the rich old men who ran the industry. The following year a public uproar broke out when the winner was revealed to be someone people considered inadequate (she was pretty average-looking and short), and their suspicions seemed to be confirmed when she started dating the geriatric chairman of the network.

So it's not that Ma meant to be cruel when she told me that I could never be Miss Hong Kong. She had her reasons. First, obviously, she didn't want me sleeping my way to success. But being "beautiful" also wasn't an attribute she considered to be important in my case. Or, for that matter, all that useful. From her personal experience, beauty, her beauty, didn't fix anything and it didn't make anything either. In Ma's mind, being beautiful only caused her to be exploited by her parents, and their neglect caused her to be violated as a young girl, and, later, resulted in her being dependent on men—first my father and then my stepfather.

I met him for the first time when Ma finally sent for me to spend the summer with her in Hong Kong a year after she and Dad broke up. I was seven. By this point, I was afraid to leave Dad. I was afraid to get on the plane by myself as an Unaccompanied Minor. But I was more afraid of who I would encounter on the other side.

A gorgeous young woman met me in the airport arrivals area. Her hair was parted in the middle, hanging down each shoulder, held back by jeweled clips on either side. This was not the tired, harried woman who worked two jobs that I

remembered. She lifted a multi-ring adorned hand. And her long red nails beckoned me forward. A glimmer of recognition. And then . . . the voice. "ELAINE!" The Squawking Chicken. My mother. I was claimed. "This is Uncle."

Ma introduced me to an older man standing next to her with benevolent eyes and a goofy expression. He had no hair and wore glasses. He was tall, taller than Dad, with a soft belly and a round face, the kind of face that ate well, drank well and never worried. Uncle tried to hug me. I resisted. He laughed, a kind laugh, and patted me on the head. "We're going to have a great summer," he told me. Then he led us to the car and drove us home, only he didn't leave. Uncle came inside too. And Uncle stayed. In Ma's bedroom.

He was an executive with an oil and gas company. When he went to work, Ma played mah-jong with the old crew. He indulged my mother's whims. He was generous with my greedy grandmother. He loaned money to her siblings. He didn't mind when Ma invited her mah-jong friends over for all-night sessions. He didn't shut himself in the TV room and smoke cigarettes, sulking about money, sulking about life's injustices. Instead, Uncle offered to go out for late-night takeout. Uncle offered to do everything. And he never seemed bothered when people teased him that Ma ran his life.

Ma met Uncle before she married Dad, while she was working in the smuggling trade, shipping Western goods into Communist China. He was almost forty years old while she was only twenty. He pursued her but she wasn't interested. Shortly after she returned to Hong Kong, they ran into each other again. She was haggard and gaunt. She was sick all the time—the bitter unhappiness of the last few years had taken its toll on her body. She locked herself in a dark room at Grandmother's house, barely eating, trying to figure out her next steps. Uncle came to visit—bringing healing herbal teas and soups, offering to take the entire family out for dinner, offering to take Ma to the doctor. Grandmother was quickly charmed. She encouraged Ma to go out with him. She practically pushed Ma out the door. Eventually,

Uncle wore her down. He had no expectations. He just wanted to make her happy. He just wanted to look after her. He just wanted to make it easy for her.

"Easy" was the magic word. It had never been easy for Ma. She was exhausted. She was twenty-nine years old and she was tired of rebuilding her life from scratch. Disillusioned by the romanticism of youth, betrayed by the lure of idealistic love, with no assets and no opportunity, with Uncle she wouldn't have to start from nothing, and this was a proposition she couldn't afford to walk away from. The Squawking Chicken was nothing if not pragmatic.

Ma was honest with Uncle. She told him that she would always love Dad. She told him that she didn't know if she could ever love him the way she loved Dad. But she promised him she would be loyal to him. She promised him she would be a good wife. She became a great asset to him professionally. She helped him navigate tricky business relationships, advising him on how to diplomatically advance through the company, cautioning him about potential enemies, encouraging him in areas where he could benefit, politically and financially. She accompanied him on business trips around Asia, a lively, pretty accessory, delighting his associates and partners. She looked after his elderly parents, supervising funeral arrangements for his mother when he was too overcome by grief to manage. He grew more and more successful with Ma at his side. And he rewarded her with luxurious gifts, trips and, most importantly, by being a wonderful stepfather to me. For a decade they were a formidable couple.

Ma, who trusted very few people, even family, especially family, grew to trust Uncle. Perhaps more than she ever trusted anyone. But over time, Uncle grew to realize that although Ma held up her end of the bargain, no matter how devoted she was to him, no matter the peaceful contentment of their life together, he would never be her One True Love. This began to eat away at him.

When I was sixteen, ten years after they hooked up, Ma found out that Uncle had been spending time with another woman. Ma first heard it from the neighbors, who casually mentioned that they'd seen a mystery woman coming in and out of the house. Then the housekeeper, Leticia, confirmed that Uncle had a female "friend" over quite often when Ma was at mah-jong. Leticia revealed to Ma that she busted Uncle on several occasions and that he'd begged her not to say anything. Ma immediately checked Uncle's passport. She realized that when he said he was on a business trip to Singapore, he had really been in Hawaii with his lady friend. She then checked the bank account. Turns out, Uncle had purchased a new Mercedes. But there was no Mercedes parked in their driveway. He'd been lavishing gifts on the other woman and depleting their savings.

Ma was furious at Uncle, but it wasn't about the money. What was worse was that, yet again, she'd been disappointed. Once again, she'd *let* herself be disappointed. She'd let herself trust a person who only let her down. And, once again, that disappointment was a result of her powerlessness. Because Ma believed she could never be independent. She had relied on Dad and he let her down. When she relied on her beauty, though it paid off for brief periods of time, it could not be relied on to bring any lasting fulfillment.

Which is why "beautiful" is not an attribute the Squawking Chicken considers to be a compliment worth giving. It's also why she didn't think beauty should be relevant to me. Because beauty wouldn't bring me what she could never achieve: independence. And Miss Hong Kong was not independent.

∂G

"So what pretty?" Ma would always tell me if I ever talked about someone's looks.

"So what pretty" was one of the Squawking Chicken's favorite expressions. She'd say it anytime I complimented a girl's looks. And she'd be extra loud about it too, with an exaggerated shrug of the shoulders, one red-nailed hand tossed off to the side, and scorn on her face.

"So what pretty? Pretty can go like this," and she'd snap her fingers and tell the Legend of Butcher Chow's Daughter.

Butcher Chow had a thriving business. He was so skilled, people from neighboring villages would walk miles just to buy from his stand. Chow was able to cut his meats in such a way that they'd be much more receptive to flavoring. If two pounds of meat from two different butchers were prepared the exact same way, Chow's pound would always taste better, time after time, because of his special slicing technique, a family secret that was passed down from his ancestors.

Butcher Chow had only one child, a daughter so pretty, so delicate he refused to teach her the family trade, believing it to be beneath her beauty. Instead, when his daughter became of age, Butcher Chow held meat-cutting competitions to find her a suitable husband to which he could pass on his coveted skill. Families sent their sons from neighboring villages far and wide in hope they not only marry the loveliest girl in the land, but also would learn a trade that would bring fortune and fame to their home.

The son of a produce merchant was the eventual winner. He was to apprentice with Chow for a year before the wedding. On the day of the groom's final lesson, he purposefully let his hand slip during a complicated maneuver. The knife went flying toward Butcher Chow's daughter, slicing open her face, and cutting off one of her fingers. It would leave a gash from her ear to her mouth.

The produce merchant now refused to marry his son to a disfigured bride. The wedding was called off. And, perhaps even worse, Butcher Chow's secret was compromised. His daughter, now with only nine fingers, was incapable of taking over his business. The produce merchant's son became a master butcher, and since his family's stall now offered produce as well as high-end meats, their business soon took over Chow's. Chow died without an heir to his legacy. And since he taught his daughter nothing, she eventually had to go work as a scullery maid in the produce merchant's household.

"So what pretty?" Without knowledge, Daughter Chow's pretty was fleeting. Deprived of a useful skill because she was pretty, Daughter Chow was dependent on others—her father, her scoundrel of a fiancé. In Ma's mind, being pretty was infinitely less serviceable than being knowledgeable.

Pretty was only useful for so long. Growing up, I was always made to cut my hair short, in a bowl. I longed to grow it out. I used to put towels over my head and pretend it was long, luscious hair because Ma kept denying my pleas, instead choosing practicality over high maintenance. The

Squawking Chicken rationale was that there was still time. "Why rushing? If you lucky enough to be pretty like Mama, why you want pretty so early? Your whole life you can be pretty. Pretty now and the people they get boring."

Instead of getting pretty, Ma preferred that I get smart. Ma never had the opportunity to develop any skills, practical, useful skills that could lift her circumstances and allow her to be self-sufficient. The Squawking Chicken, like Daughter Chow, was a great beauty too. But because she never finished high school, all that was left for her was work that was demeaning. Even beautiful girls have to do shitty work. But Ma was determined that my work would not be shitty. Ma was determined that my work would not be based on appearance but on my mind. Education was the priority. For both me and my dad, but no longer for her. She felt that her window of opportunity had closed. So she transferred her ambitions to both of us.

Ma divorcing my father was the impetus he needed to get going. She'd taken off without me. He was now responsible for me. He could no longer spend his evenings smoking in front of the television, lamenting his fate and feeling sorry for himself. And Dad took Ma at her word. *I will come back to you if you make something of yourself.*

He was working an office job in the accounting department at a computer company when he and Ma divorced.

There was opportunity there to advance. Dad took on extra work on the weekends to make money for tuition fees. In the evenings he'd go to night school. It took three years. Three years of no rest, not a day to spare, no downtime, no relaxing, just work and school, work and school, saving, saving, saving, so that somehow there was enough money to send me to private school, one of the best in Toronto. Eventually Dad became a Certified General Accountant and rose within the company. He was tenacious, he was now educated and he was making something of himself. Ma expected this of me too.

There's a joke in my family that you're nothing if you don't have at least two jobs. Ma had two jobs when she immigrated to Canada. Dad had two jobs as an immigrant, not unlike many immigrants who find themselves in a new country, shocked by a new culture, but with no time to indulge in feeling sorry for themselves. Survival comes first. Survival comes before feelings. You do what you need to do to get it done. You work as many jobs as you can, and you go to school, and you raise a child, and you don't complain. Who has time to complain anyway? Immigrants of my parents' generation were too busy to complain.

This is the immigrant philosophy Ma used to guide me. Hard work is all there is. Hard work produces results. Pretty does not produce results. Neither does being special.

Modern Western parents tell their kids they're special all the time. For many modern Western parents, telling a child she is neither pretty nor special is harsh and cruel. For the Squawking Chicken, telling me I was neither pretty nor special was just about getting real. And it was her duty as my mother to get real with me. "Mama will always tell you the truth. Mama will never lie to you. I am the only one. Sometimes the truth hurts. But the truth will also protect you. I am not here to be nice to you. I am here to protect you."

Ma was protecting me from silly dreams. Dreams that were unattainable. Dreams that were a waste of time. Ma killed my dreams often. She killed the dreams that she knew were impossible, dreams based on attributes I didn't have. Like becoming Miss Hong Kong when I was eleven years old. Sure, maybe it's harmless, letting a young girl fantasize about beauty pageants. For the Squawking Chicken, though, setting a child up for disappointment by allowing her to believe in impossible dreams is the ultimate failure of a parent. In the Squawking Chicken's mind, the parent who allows her child to dream the impossible dream is the parent who is doing her child a great disservice. As she says, the parent who tells her child that even her shit smells good is the parent who'll end up picking up her child's shit when she grows up.

Ma made that comment once when we were on a holiday

cruise together in 1996. Back then, there was an assigned dinner seating plan for every guest on board. This meant that we'd share each meal with the same people for the duration of the cruise. Our dining partners were a young couple with a daughter, around three or four years old. She was an active girl, and she was constantly twirling and jumping. According to her parents, she loved dancing. She danced through the entire first dinner, at one point knocking over Ma's water. The girl's mother apologized, but didn't stop her daughter's leg-kicking, explaining, "She's so good at it, we don't want to discourage her."

This went on for a few days. And every time the child would stumble, or cause a minor accident from her flailing, the parents would behave like she was the next Anna Pavlova who simply could not be stopped. Ma was not impressed. After a particularly eventful dinner, during which Anna Pavlova Jr. had tripped over her own feet, hitting her head on the corner of the table, and wailing for the next hour, Ma had had enough. "She dance? You're sure?"

The amazing thing is that they didn't actually process what Ma was saying. They just kept repeating the mantra: *She just loves to dance! We couldn't stop her if we tried!* Ma was properly disgusted when we left the dining room. "They clap when she falls. They clap when she farts. People are going to point and laugh at that girl when she grows up. You watch. All because they keep letting her think she's so special."

We are living in a culture of "special." Evidence of this is all over prime-time television. Every off-tune *American Idol* hopeful is told he or she is special, indulged in the pursuit of a reality that happens for very, very few people. Like Anna Pavlova Jr. We never saw Anna Pavlova Jr. and her parents again after the cruise but I can promise you she never became a dancer, even though her parents would have kept encouraging it.

Ma refused to encourage me in areas where she knew I could not succeed. Ma believed that Anna Pavlova Jr.'s parents' insistence on her (lack of) dancing ability would only set her up for failure and disappointment. So the Squawking Chicken never let me believe I was special. Instead she encouraged me to pursue dreams that could be realized on my own actual, tangible strengths: tenacity, curiosity, an aptitude for communication.

Not surprisingly, she was also very stingy with praise. "Why you need so many compliments? Why you not satisfied for doing a good job? Do I need to throw a party every time you fart?" This was her way of never letting me get too high. Though I was rewarded now and again for good marks—

with mah-jong chips or allowance bonuses—Ma never flattered me excessively, if at all. The Squawking Chicken was always my reality check.

For the same reason she checked me for not being special, she also checked me for needing to celebrate my achievements. It's the immigrant mentality: there's no time to celebrate yourself, there's always more to do. Ma was happy when I did well, when I brought home a good score on a test. But her praise was measured, never over the top. Because she never wanted me to coast and boast. And if I ever did boast, well, Mrs. Chiang would come for a visit.

Every Chinese kid must have a Mrs. Chiang. Mrs. Chiang is the Chinese way of motivating your kids. Because Mrs. Chiang's kid was always the gold standard. Mrs. Chiang's kid reminded you that you still had a long way to go. Mrs. Chiang's kid reminded me after acing a math test in Grade 7 that this wasn't all that big of a deal.

It was March break and I was visiting Ma in Hong Kong. We were at Grandmother's mah-jong den, as usual, and Dad had called to tell me that my math results had arrived in the mail—93 percent, among the highest in the class.

As soon as I put down the phone, I announced the news to Ma and all the aunties. Everyone was really proud of me. Ma gave me a one-hundred-dollar chip. With the exchange rate then, it would have amounted to twenty dollars. I was thrilled. Not only had Ma complimented me, she also publicly rewarded me. That almost never happened. So I decided to milk it for all it was worth. I went on and on about myself. I bragged about how smart I was. I bragged about how no one else in the class was able to understand the math concepts as quickly as I did. I bragged about how easy that exam was. I bragged about how quickly I finished. I could not stop bragging.

Until Ma decided it was time to check me with Mrs. Chiang. She turned to the auntie playing to her right, the one sitting closest to me: "Mrs. Chiang's daughter is a doctor now. What a hardworking, humble girl. So conscientious! Five years and she didn't even go out once, not even to see a movie. And now she's a doctor at the big hospital. Mrs. Chiang is so lucky. Poor me. All I got was a girl who did well on one test. So what? One test and she's shaking her ass all over the block. Mrs. Chiang's daughter is healing people and saving lives. My daughter just knows how to shake her ass." Looking into my eyes now, "Shake your ass when you show me your doctor's diploma. Otherwise, don't bother me. I can't concentrate on the game."

Mrs. Chiang's daughter is the reason why I rarely pause to celebrate my wins. As of this writing, I have three jobs.

It's been seven years since my last real holiday. Last summer Ma called while I was out playing a round of golf on a rare light Friday afternoon. Golf is a long game. It was five hours later when I called her back.

"That was almost the whole day," she observed. "Are you working this weekend?" Ma will never let me coast.

CHAPTER 7

Don't Cut Bangs over Thirty

The first thing I do when I wake up is lubricate my eyes with eye drops. Then I boil water and drink hot water throughout the day. I also eat a papaya every day. And an orange. My husband starts his day the same way. Eye drops, hot water, but the difference is that he eats a banana.

This is not a habit. This is not by preference. This routine comes by order from the Squawking Chicken. And it has everything to do with feng shui.

"Feng" means wind in Chinese. "Shui" is water. When the wind blows in the right direction, when the water flows toward the right places, life is in balance, harmony is achieved, and conditions are ideal for happiness and prosperity. The goal of feng shui is to find the most auspicious wind-water formula. And the formula for each person is different; we are born to different parents, in different years, during different months, at different times of day, in different locations, and these differences mean that different variables can affect our individual wind-water dynamics.

Feng shui is an ancient practice. Over the centuries, feng shui has evolved from its original principles, modifying and expanding with the evolution of Chinese culture, influenced by local traditions, social advancements and then interpreted, sometimes indiscriminately, by modern feng shui masters. Feng shui books are now sold in Asian markets like almanacs, with some people preferring one master over the other, eagerly waiting for the New Year to learn their fates over the next year, and the recommendations made so that they can adjust their own wind-water equations to either boost success or prevent calamity.

Adherence to feng shui is not unlike devotion to religion. There are certain standard commandments. Every sin, or deliberate rejection of a feng shui commandment, carries a consequence. Redemption is not impossible, but sacrifices must be made. The nonbelievers are regarded with compassion and pity. They cannot be saved.

The Squawking Chicken is a devout believer. And, much like a pious Christian might be drawn to Jesus as a way of coping with the unpredictable, often devastating currents of life, as a way to explain and accept tragedy and in the hope of mitigating future misfortune, Ma embraced feng shui. To Ma, feng shui defends her against the sadness and betrayal that seems to follow her. It helps her manage expectations about future disappointments. And it guides me so that I might not only avoid the same experiences but be in a position to have better ones. For feng shui isn't so much a path to good luck, but a way to open oneself to the arrival of good luck and, more importantly, to prepare for the inevitable onset of bad luck.

Ma has structured my life around feng shui principles for the same reason she told me ghost stories instead of reading princess fairy tales when I was a child. Because no one has to be prepared in advance for when great things are about to happen. There's nothing to worry about when great things are about to happen. But you should worry when shit goes down. And shit *will* always go down. No one rides a winning streak forever.

Everything the Squawking Chicken taught me—values, morality, discipline—was a result of her own personal brand of feng shui combined with Chinese astrology and fortune-telling. The first time she directly applied her feng shui/astrology/fortune-telling hybrid to my life it was on my face. Almost right after I got off the plane in Hong Kong the summer I was eight, she noticed the mole between my eyes. It was small but she stared at it for days like she was trying to make it grow. She insisted it had grown very quickly, claiming it was much less visible three months earlier when I was in Hong Kong for spring break. Grandmother and all the mah-jong aunties waved it off, said she was crazy and that they could barely see it. But Ma was obsessed. She was convinced it would keep getting larger and she kept flipping through her feng shui almanac, to a page with sketches of faces and arrows pointing to certain areas of the face, and then looking at my face, comparing it to the drawings.

The following week she made up her mind. She was taking me to the doctor to get rid of the mole. I didn't want to go. I was just at that age where I'd started becoming vain. I worried that removing the mole would leave a major scar. Ma brushed off my concerns. She told me that the scar would heal quickly, that eventually I'd barely be able to find it, especially after the stitches came out. Stitches?! That made it even worse. So I'd be walking around with string sticking out of my face? But there was no arguing with her. I had no choice. Dr. Tang would take care of it. He cut into the space between my eyebrows, just above my nose, and dug that fucker out with Ma in the room right beside him, watching everything. To be honest, it didn't hurt. I can barely remember the experience. But Ma was triumphant for days. Wherever we went, she gave a play-by-play of my mole removal, describing it in graphic detail.

According to her, the mole was a monster below the surface. While it was tiny and unremarkable on my face, underneath it was the size of a fat sesame seed. Ma described Dr. Tang's surprise at its depth, after he had painstakingly made an incision around it. She gave the mole a personality, and said it seemed determined to stay inside, that its root was strong and stubborn, and that Dr. Tang had to delicately dig around in there in order to be able to, in the end, successfully tweeze it out. The way Ma told the story, the mole seemed like a parasite and she was its conqueror, protecting me from its eventual domination over my face.

"You should have seen it, Ah Leuy! You should have seen it!" she'd repeat excitedly. "What we saw was just the tip of the volcano. And it would have kept rising! In a few years, that thing would have been spreading all over the place. You'd be a freak if it wasn't for Mama."

But the truth was that Ma wasn't worried about the aesthetics of the mole. Her primary concern was my life, or, rather, my death. According to her feng shui almanac, someone with a mole in that position would die a premature death at the age of twenty-two by drowning. That's the creepy thing about feng shui—it's very specific. Uncomfortably specific.

Ma only revealed to me the reason she was so obsessed with killing my mole after Dr. Tang had taken it out. She showed me the feng shui face-mapping pages in her almanac, pointing to the diagrams and Chinese words I didn't understand, explaining that our lives follow a certain path on our faces. And that our features can dictate our fates and also our futures.

Ma has a mole on the right side of her chin, just above her jawline. When I asked her why she kept it after having mine removed, she said that a mole in that area meant that person would have "mouth luck"—eat well, speak well—but only until they're sixty years old. At the age of sixty, the mole would lose its power. Ma was sixty when she was hospitalized for nine months with a rare illness called POEMS syndrome: polyneuropathy (peripheral nerve damage), organomegaly (abnormal enlargement of organs), endocrinopathy (damage to hormone-producing glands) or edema, M protein (an abnormal immunoglobulin) and skin abnormalities.

It actually started about eighteen months before her sixtieth birthday. Ma started feeling weak for no reason. Every night, around the same time, she'd feel numbness in her left arm. And she was losing weight. Just two pounds a month initially and then more and more until she was emaciated, just ninety-five pounds. At the time she was admitted to the hospital, it was three weeks after she turned sixty. By this point, she was unable to walk, paralyzed from the waist down, and her hands and fingers were starting to go too. She was examined by several specialists. They were baffled by

her symptoms, continually ruling out one disease after another. Finally, after two months in the hospital, they diagnosed her with POEMS and began treatment. Ma began to
recover and was eventually transferred to a rehabilitation
hospital to begin learning how to walk again. While there,
she met the only other POEMS patient in the Toronto
area. The woman was a year older than the Squawking
Chicken. Her POEMS symptoms were almost identical to
Ma's, only they started a year earlier. And she too had a mole
on the right side of her chin, just above her jawline.

Moles aren't the only facial characteristics that can affect
our lives and personalities. When I was growing up, Ma
would constantly drop her face-mapping wisdom into our
conversations, especially when we were people watching.
We have all been unfair judgy bitches when it comes to criticizing people's appearances. Ma justified her judgy bitchi-
ness with fortune-telling and face-mapping. A man might
walk into a restaurant, the whites of his eyes more prominent than the dark center. If the end of his eyebrows are
higher than the start of his eyebrows, even with a slight cur-
vature, he's deemed a pervert, and she'll glare at him through
the course of the entire meal, alerting everyone around that
we're in the midst of a rapist. If a woman's mouth is too
wide, it could be a problem too. This is generally considered
an attractive feature in the Western world. For the Squawk-

ing Chicken, a wide-mouthed woman, with all that space around her teeth, can't be trusted, because she always wants to fit too much in, and in trying to be everything to everyone, she can't have a solid sense of herself.

I never liked my nose. I always complained about it. My nose is a slightly less pronounced version of Ma's nose. It's a hook nose with a bump at the top that curves downward and, in my mind, looks sort of like a hawk's. Or a chicken. Some kind of fowl. Ma loves her nose, and whenever I'd bitch about my nose, wishing it was smaller, narrower, pointier at the end and slightly turned up, she'd tell me I was stupid. That having a nose like mine was better than having a nose with "no meat." Women with no-meat noses bring bad luck to their men. Whenever we'd see a woman with a no-meat nose, Ma would shake her head and feel sorry for the husband. "That poor man will slave away his whole life and because of his wife's empty nose, it will never be enough. He will always come up short."

A lifetime of listening to the Squawking Chicken judge people by facial fortunes has affected the way I see people too. We have a friend, Jon, who brought around a new girlfriend. Everyone liked her immediately except for me, even though she was lovely. I could not bring myself to warm to her. At home later that night, my husband asked me why I was so unfriendly to Jon's girlfriend at the party. I had no legitimate reason, other than the fact that she had a no-meat nose. Which to me meant that she was wrong for Jon because her no-meat nose would never be fulfilled. I would not be nice to a girl with an empty, no-meat nose who'd bring bad luck to my friend. (Jon ended up marrying someone else a few years later. Her nose had more meat on it.)

More and more, Ma started imposing her feng shui and face-mapping beliefs on my appearance just like she did with my mole. I was only eight when the mole came out, too young to refuse. As I got older, with a stronger will, Ma couldn't just drag me to the doctor's clinic whenever she detected a physical flaw in my face fortune. Then again, the mole scare was the groundwork. That incident in combination with all her other ghost/feng shui/fortune-telling stories began to make me more and more superstitious. And this is how she has manipulated me to this day, a formally educated, rational adult, into doing whatever she wants me to do, even when there's no actual scientific reason for it.

I call it Feng Shui Blackmail.

Feng Shui Blackmail is why I can't wear bangs. According to Chinese fortune-telling and face-mapping, our fates and our luck can be foretold on our faces. My mole predicted an early death by drowning. And so it was removed. While certain features can portend disaster, other features have the opposite effect. They can attract luck and, even more significant, they can protect you from bad luck. Remember, the goal of feng shui and noble fortune-telling is not necessarily to profit from good luck but to harvest it, so that it can be relied upon to counter the inevitable valleys in life, those times when opportunities are scarce, and things don't come quite so easily.

The forehead is one of the most prominent features of the human face. When we lower our heads, our foreheads lead us forward. In fortune-telling then, the forehead is our natural shield and warrior. It is the source of our fire, from where we draw the strength to guard ourselves and from where we fight. The Chinese believe that the forehead holds three flames. When we are lucky, our foreheads are bright—they glow. Our positive energy from within is reflected on the outside on our forehead "shields," fueling the three flames. It is imperative to keep those flames stoked. They must be able to burn, unencumbered, as representations of our light. That way they can guard us, guard our luck, guard our resources. Ma always reminded me that if I were going somewhere that might be full of bad energy, like a hospital full of sick people and spirits, or to a funeral home, where death never leaves, to always wear my hair back, to make sure my forehead was at full power, those three soldier flames ready for battle.

Those three flames can't be effective when they're covered, then, right? Cutting bangs would be cock-blocking their force. Cutting bangs is like snuffing them out. They'd be paralyzed and incapable of defending you. If they can't defend you, you have to then deplete your energy and luck reserves, valuable commodities you might need later.

Each time I cut bangs, my luck was indeed diminished. Pimples erupted all over my forehead, and sometimes even lower, on my cheeks and chin, the ashes of those three flames scattered across the battlefield of my face. Each time I did it without consulting the Squawking Chicken. Each time she was unsympathetic. "Look at you. I told you about bangs. So now, not only are you ugly, you're not even lucky."

It's true. I wasn't lucky during my bangs phases. Even though I loved the way they looked, the way they framed my eyes, gave them some mystery and intrigue, the zits weren't exactly making me more attractive, and I found that I wasn't as quick with my studies, I wasn't as happy with my friends, I didn't have as much money to spend.

The last time I had bangs I was twenty-two years old. And it wasn't bangs, exactly, but I had cut my hair very short, in a pixie style, and was trying to grow it out so that the front part of my hair was like bangs, with nowhere else to fall but into my forehead. I broke out. And I had a boyfriend at the time—with a mother who hated me. One night, when he brought me to dinner, his mother said to me, in front of his entire family: "You should eat more fruit. It might help with your skin problem."

I was mortified. He broke up with me a few weeks after that. Sure, we weren't right for each other in the end, but that meddling mother of his wasn't helping. I partly blame her and I partly blame those fucking bangs. I haven't had bangs ever since . . . though I considered it, in my late twenties, only now I was wiser and asked Ma about it first. This time, she came at it a different way. "You are approaching thirty. It is a time in your life when you have the most potential. It is time to strike. It is time to push, hard, for the next decade, to set yourself up for when you start to age and slow down. Never cut bangs in your thirties. Never go into your thirties with the three flames at half their potency or less. Why would you handicap yourself? Why would you risk that? Don't say I didn't warn you."

Why jeopardize your future for a goddamn hairstyle?

Feng Shui Blackmail.

Sometimes, though, Feng Shui Blackmail can make you look like a real dick. Ma was reading my Chinese horoscope a few years ago. She said that my luck was good, but fragile. That I had to be careful because my luck, while generally favorable, was vulnerable to attack from sinister forces. I was to stay away from hospitals and funeral homes, especially funeral homes. Under no circumstances was I to attend a funeral, preferably ever, unless it was a very close family member. And it had to be *close*.

The Funeral Policy is still in effect. And I am super stressed about it. Because, well, you never know. And God forbid, if something shitty were to happen to one of my friends, I'd want to be there for them. I don't want to be the asshole who doesn't support a friend just because I'm worried about my luck. Whenever I try to discuss this conundrum with the Squawking Chicken, she always answers the same way. "You go to the funeral, you will get back luck. Why you want to bring bad luck on your friend? This is very stupid. Why do your friends want such a stupid friend?"

There are times, though, when I suspect that Ma blackmails me not for any legitimate fortune-telling/good-luck/bad-luck–feng shui reasons, but simply because she just doesn't like something I'm wearing. I'll be in a dress, for example, and she'll hate the style, so she'll tell me that I might not do as well in my meetings, and not be as lucky, because the dress color is unlucky. I'll wear the same color a week later, in a different cut, and she'll be all over it. "You looks good." Now that I'm on television, she is particularly critical of my clothing and appearance choices. If it's a lip color she's not fond of, that lip color will automatically mean I'll screw up my lines. If my blouse isn't to her preference, it'll be the cause of my missing my cues.

And still, *still*, even though I know it's probably nothing to do with actual luck, she has manipulated me so successfully through Feng Shui Blackmail that I'll change anyway. I will take off the unlucky trousers and replace them with a pair we both agree on. I will adjust my jacket until she approves. And when she approves, I'll go on the air with that much more confidence. Because the Squawking Chicken said it was lucky. So how could it possibly not be?

Feng Shui Blackmail is the reason I was married on a Friday, a year before Jacek and I had planned on actually getting married. He proposed in October 2000. We wanted to take our time in planning the wedding. We hoped to do it in 2002. Six months after Jacek proposed, Ma called me late in the evening. She'd been studying her fortune-telling books and looking at her feng shui calendar, comparing my birth coordinates to Jacek's. I was born in 1973, the year of the Ox. Jacek was born in 1975, making him a Rabbit. There was a lucky day that was coming up very soon, much sooner than we were initially prepared for. Ma pressed upon us the auspiciousness of the date. She said it was the perfect date. She said it was the most ideal day to begin our life together. She insisted that we seriously consider moving the wedding up by an entire year so that we could take advantage of this day. It was November 2, 2001, a Friday, and the ceremony had to happen between eleven and one o'clock in the afternoon.

Jacek was new to all this Chinese feng shui business. He comes from a Polish background. His father is an engineer, his mother an architect. Feng shui isn't their thing. So he was understandably mystified by all this culture shock that was coming his way. It's not that he wasn't willing to push up our wedding, it's that he was totally confused by the reason for it.

That's how feng shui is—it cannot be explained, at least not scientifically. I told him about a friend of ours who really wanted to get married on a certain day because it was a Saturday on a good weekend in the fall. She was able to secure her favorite venue, ignoring the caution that came from the fortune-teller her family had hired to calculate the luckiness or unluckiness of that particular date. The fortune-teller warned that the marriage would be disastrous if they went ahead with it. The fortune-teller offered other options. Our friend dismissed them all. She and her groom were married on the day of her choice. And they were divorced six weeks later.

Jacek was like, okay, yeah, but he was cheating on her, that would still have happened even if they picked another day. Would it have? The prediction that that day was cursed came true. And if it wouldn't kill us to get married a year earlier, why not go with it, especially when we were lucky enough to get a day that was so lucky for us?

We were married on the morning of November 2, 2001, at eleven o'clock in Vancouver. It rains a lot in Vancouver, especially during that time of year. It had rained overnight, it was raining that morning when I woke up, and the forecast called for rain the rest of the day. An hour before our ceremony, though, the clouds drifted away. The sky was clear. It was actually sunny for the next four hours, in time for us to exchange vows, take pictures and return to the shelter of our hotel, at which point the rain returned. Coincidence or feng shui fortune-telling?

Jacek was starting to come around, but he was still confused from time to time. Sometimes it was due to language. Like he didn't understand why my dad kept giving him pants. The word for "pants" in Chinese is *fu*. It's pronounced in Cantonese exactly the same as the word for "wealth." We Chinese do this a lot with our words—when they sound similar, we attach their meanings, even if their actual meanings have nothing to do with each other.

For example, the word for the number four sounds sort of like the word for "death." They're two entirely different characters (in English that would be the equivalent of two totally different spellings) but close phonetically; one is just delivered in a lower register. Because of their similar sounds, the number four is considered to be the unluckiest number in Chinese culture. This is why there is never a fourth floor or a fourteenth floor in a Chinese building, have you noticed? They skip the number entirely, not unlike the way thirteen is often avoided in Western culture.

So the reason my dad kept giving Jacek pants was because he was symbolically passing on to his son-in-law his *fu*, or his "wealth," in the form of . . . trousers. They weren't the most stylish trousers. At least not for our generation. But Jacek kept stacking them in the closet during the first two years of our marriage like he was stacking cash. He didn't quite get it, necessarily, but they kept coming, so he kept saving.

Jacek's feng shui epiphany came in the spring of 2002. Ma called to say that she was sending Dad over from Toronto to spend time with us in Vancouver on his own. Dad was born in the year of the Rat. The opposing sign of the Rat is the Horse. It was the year of the Horse and according to the almanac, Rats were passing through a shitty cycle. The almanac suggested that in the early part of May that year, Rats would be well advised to stay away from home, go on holiday. Ma told Dad to go visit us while she stayed back. We had a great time with Dad. We took time off from work and drove over to Vancouver Island, booking a town house on the water, and Dad went whale watching and for jogs along the beach. On our last day there, Ma phoned to tell us that there was something wrong with the car. She was driving it to the mall and on the way there, one of the front tires came off. It was a freak accident but she was okay. She drives really slowly and she doesn't take the highway so when it happened, she wasn't hurt and neither was anyone else. But the thing is, if Dad had been home, he would have been behind the wheel, and he would have been on the highway at top speed. He would not have been so lucky. Except . . . he was. Because he had left town. My parents and I were convinced that Dad had avoided disaster. Jacek too. He was now a full-fledged believer. And the Squawking Chicken took full advantage.

She stepped up her Feng Shui Blackmail after the wedding. It started with a simple suggestion: start your day with hot water and keep it up throughout. Hot water is the beverage of choice for old Chinese ladies. They believe there are certain health benefits. Water of course is good for you, no matter the culture. Hot water, as opposed to cold water, however, warms up your energy, it fires up your spirit, it's pure, it's sterile. But Ma's insistence on drinking hot water was for more than just good health. As always, it was about feng shui and fortune-telling and it had magical properties that she was reluctant to explain.

There are those who maintain that revealing the secrets behind feng shui and fortune-telling will weaken their enchantments. Part of their power comes from blind devotion. If you trust, without question, without justification, they will reward you for your loyalty. Ma was of the mind that the more she divulged about the workings of feng shui and fortune-telling, the less effective her methods would be because she would be betraying an ancient code, something else she's never been very forthcoming about. The point is you just have to believe. That's it. And if you don't believe, well, you'll see. That's Feng Shui Blackmail: the "or else" is always implied.

Whenever I'd ask, "But why? What's going to happen if I don't [do whatever weird voodoo it is that you're telling me to do]?" she'd just wave me off, impatiently, almost angrily: "I don't want to say . . . but it's up to you." The "or else" would hang there, over my head, like an upside-down jack-in-the-box just waiting to pop out and fuck me up. Though she'll never confirm it, I suspect the hot water has something to do with money. In Cantonese, "water" is slang for "money." Kind of like the word "bucks" in English means "dollars." A hundred bucks equals a hundred dollars. In Cantonese we say, "One block of water equals a hundred dollars." So you never want to have a leak in your house, and if you do, you'd better take care of it as soon as possible. Otherwise, you're losing money. My assumption then is that Ma's hot water obsession has to do with us replenishing our money supply. Whenever I bring it up, she always changes the subject.

So we drink the water almost religiously.

About three months after she had us adopting the water routine, she commanded that we start lubricating our eyes, preferably as soon as we woke up. Ma was more accommodating about providing answers to this one. She explained to us that our eyes are the source of our wisdom and decision-making ability. The eye drops were nutrition for the eyes. They would make them clearer, and that would make "seeing" a lot smoother so that we could identify trouble more efficiently and opportunity more often. Eye drops is what I get for my birthday. A supersize box from Costco—this is my annual gift. And that's it. And when I complain about how that's a shitty present, the Squawking Chicken counters with, "My present will make your eyes stronger, and if your eyes are stronger, you will be more successful. How is a sweater going to make you more successful? Why are you such an ingrate?"

So we moisten our eyes almost religiously.

The eye drops were followed by the papayas a year later. We were to both start eating papayas. Ma wouldn't divulge whatever it was that made papayas so special for us. "I'm telling you. Just eat the papayas. Stop asking questions."

Papayas aren't exactly the most economical fruit. So at first, Jacek and I would halve them. When Ma found out we were halving them, she asked us how much we were paying every time we went to play golf. "For ten measly dollars, you're skimping on papayas? Don't say I didn't tell you when you . . . you know."

"What?"

"You know."

"What?" Nothing. End of discussion. Feng Shui Blackmail works every time.

So my husband and I stopped halving our papayas and started eating one each. About a year into our papaya eating, my gossip business began gaining momentum. Two years into our papaya eating, my gossip blog caught the attention of the producers at *Etalk*, a Canadian entertainment news show. Though I had no television experience, I was offered a part-time position as a reporter. Six months later they gave me a contract. It was 2006 and with both the television gig and my blog, celebrity gossip, my passion, also became my dream career. Three years into our papaya eating, Jacek quit his job at a telecommunications company and managed the administrative and sales side of our gossip blog full-time. I was, by this point, completely reliant on papayas. No day was complete without a papaya. A day without a papaya was a day that would certainly turn out to be less-than . . . even though, frankly, I don't like papayas. I don't like the taste. I don't like the texture. And they're a pain in the ass. You have to scoop out the seeds. It's messy. It's not a wash-and-go fruit.

One day, during one of our several daily calls, Ma asked me if I'd eaten my papaya yet. It was midafternoon. And I was putting it off. I sighed, like it was a drag. First she reminded me that my papaya should ideally be consumed before six o'clock so as to maximize its effectiveness through the day. Then she asked me what my problem was. I told her that the flavor wasn't the best. That papayas weren't my favorite. That I regarded the eating of papayas as a necessary chore, like a visit to the dentist.

The Squawking Chicken sighed back, never a good thing. I panicked. I thought it was over. I worried I had just pissed away all my good luck. I thought maybe something might happen to me—a car accident, a backstabbing, Lindsay Lohan suing me for repeatedly calling her an asshole . . .

"What's wrong? Am I going to be okay?????" I pleaded down the phone line.

"Yes. You will be fine. You could be better though. But the papaya can't help you to its full capacity if you're not fully committed."

That's what a bitch feng shui and fortune-telling can be.

Not only do you have to follow it, you have to fucking enjoy it at the same time.

Eventually, however, my papaya requirement became a problem on the road, legitimately. As a television correspondent, travel was a big part of the job. And papayas aren't the kind of fruit that can be found at every ordinary grocery store. Papayas are not apples. Papayas aren't even pineapples. When I presented this dilemma to the Squawking Chicken, she asked me to give her some time to think of a solution. Eventually she recommended oranges. This is when I realized that color might have something to do with it. Papayas and oranges are the same color. By now, though, I knew enough not to verbalize my hypothesis. (At least not until now. Some things are best not said out loud. Saying them out loud might jinx it. Which is why I have serious anxiety about writing this chapter. If this book ends up bombing, I'll know exactly why.)

Anyway, oranges became a substitute. Papayas are still the best, but oranges will do in a pinch. Some days, when I need some extra juju, I'll have both.

But papayas and oranges aren't for everyone. Papayas were specifically chosen for my coordinates, my sign, my particular energy. Jacek, for example, has since transitioned off papayas and over to bananas. In 2009, the Squawking

Chicken declared that he was to add bananas to his routine and that he could drop the papaya. I love bananas. I was jealous. I asked if I could have bananas too.

"If you want to. But for you, bananas will never be as good as papayas. Don't look at me if you figure that out too late."

I could not have written this book without papayas.

But the Feng Shui Blackmail of hot water, eye drops, and daily fruit is nothing compared to the Feng Shui Blackmail restrictions of house hunting. The home is the center of people's lives. Feng shui guidelines in home selection and home interiors are very specific. You see this in the Western real estate market—the industry is becoming more and more savvy as the Chinese continue to invest in properties around the world.

Eight is the luckiest number in Chinese numerology. It's that pronunciation thing again. *Baht* is how you said the word for "eight" in Cantonese. It rhymes with *faht*, the word for "rich." So an eight is synonymous with getting rich, getting lucky. This is why real estate agents often end their list prices with the number eight. This is why Chinese people often send back their counteroffers with amounts that include at least one eight. If a house is listed at $299,400, a prospective Chinese buyer might send back a counter of $299,388. You see what I did there? Four is normally regarded as an unlucky number. It's been replaced here with a couple of eights.

This is just a generalization though. As it is with the fruit, we all have our own lucky numbers. A couple of years ago, Jacek started seeing fours all over the place. He'd look at the clock, it was 4:44. He'd buy something, it would amount to $14.44. Or $24.44. He was freaking out. So much so that he asked Ma whether or not he was in for it. She assured him that it would be okay. That the fours that were surrounding him were protecting him. That he was one of those rare people for whom fours were lucky. After all, he was born on April first, the first day of the fourth month. Me, I don't have a super-lucky number like Jacek. But I do have a very unlucky one. It is five. I generally avoid fives.

Chinese numerology became a big deal for us when we were looking for a home. We had sold our small apartment on West 4th Avenue (see? Jacek is drawn to fours) in Vancouver in the early part of 2008. We decided to rent while we took our time waiting for the perfect place to come up. A couple months later, we had our hearts set on a town house by the beach. It was ideal. But we had to consult with the Squawking Chicken first about the offer "number." She recommended an amount slightly under asking, with a complicated series of numbers that added up to something we didn't understand. And she would not move from that amount. We tried telling her that the market was so competitive that there was no way we would get it with that amount. Very calmly, she assured us that if we didn't get it, it wasn't ours to begin with.

Jacek was becoming frustrated. He was really into this house. He felt handcuffed by her "crazy" Feng Shui Blackmail. But as much as I wanted my husband to be happy, I also wanted to protect our happiness. The wrong house can ruin lives. The right house can enhance the lives of those living there. I wanted our home to have good energy. I trusted that Ma knew how to help us find the kind of energy we needed. I asked Jacek not to compromise our energy, our spirit, our hot streak for the sake of a piece of real estate that happened to have a good view of the city and an awesome basement that he could turn into a man cave. He eventually agreed. In the end, we lost out on that house.

That fall, the world economy collapsed. We would have overpaid on that house. Jacek just shook his head.

A couple of years passed and we checked out another town house in a development right by a park that we thought would be great for our dogs. We saw the for-sale sign one day just as the owner was outside doing some work. He agreed to show us around. It was a corner unit with a black spiked gate and chimes hanging on the porch. Inside there were three levels. The entire top level was the master bedroom. It was an oddly shaped room, with weirdly angled corners and a sloped ceiling. A hot tub took up most of the backyard. The place needed some work but we were interested so we told our agent to look into it. The day after I started feeling unwell. I was tired all the time. I felt nauseated. I couldn't eat. Ma saw me on TV a few days later and called me straightaway. "You okay? What's wrong with you? I just watched you on television and your forehead looks dark. You have no life in your eyes. Did you do something?"

I told her I wasn't sleeping well. She muttered something about taking better care of myself and hung up. The next day it was the same. She said I looked like shit on TV, insisting that I go to the doctor.

At the end of the week, our real estate agent came back to us with some more information about the town house. We always consulted both sets of parents about our home searches, so Jacek emailed the pictures to his mom and my dad and asked them what they thought. The phone rang almost immediately. It was the Squawking Chicken. She was very concerned. "Did you go into that house? Did you step inside that house?" I said that we ran into the owner and ended up getting a tour. She flipped out. "The house is dirty! That house is very dirty!"

I remembered how sinister those spikes seemed on that black gate and the sound of the chimes as we walked in—not exactly welcoming. I remembered how uncomfortable it felt upstairs, in that bedroom with the strange dimensions. I passed on these observations to the Squawking Chicken. "Bah," she spat over the phone. "I could tell just from the pictures. There is filth in there. You should have showed me before you went in."

She warned me to never again go see a house without telling her, without at least showing her some photos. So I'd been infected by a bad house. And why not Jacek? Just as certain fruits and numbers are lucky for certain people, certain forces, helpful and harmful, are attracted to others. For the evil influences swirling around that home, I was the one.

So now what?

Ma wasn't too worried. I had been eating my papayas. I was riding steady on my luck cycle due to the fact that she had spent years feng shui voodooing my ass, insulating me from exactly these kinds of occurrences. Part of that voodoo involves getting my blood taken annually after Chinese New Year. I've been doing this since 2006, when I started working for myself. Ma was concerned that success would expose me to greater dangers. As usual, she wouldn't explain what she had seen or read in my fortune that supported her theory, but she was particularly preoccupied with my health and physical well-being. So she added another ritual to the growing list of feng shui fortune-telling tasks. Jacek and I were both to "shed blood" by submitting to a blood test—for cholesterol, for creatinine, for pregnancy, whatever the reason the doctor checked off on his form, she didn't care, so long as we lost some blood. By voluntarily "shedding blood" we were preempting something that could be much more serious. It's kind of like a sacrifice, only without major consequences. (By the way, a dental appointment works too. Because when you get your teeth cleaned, there's inevitably a small amount of bleeding.)

Since I had dutifully given of my blood that year, Ma was confident that my luck was at a decent level and that I could recover quickly from the dirty house. She advised me to get my hair cut right away. She wanted at least three inches off the length. I have very long hair, halfway down my back. And I don't like it any shorter. But Ma convinced me that I needed to purge. That the only way I'd rid myself of the darkness, the negative energy that the house had left on me, was to release it through the ends of my hair. It was holding me down. I had three inches taken off and immediately felt better.

Our house search continued. I don't think we were any more or less picky than any other home buyers, but we did have one condition that complicated the process: the staircase. Many town houses are designed with the staircase facing the front door. Ordinarily this is considered to be bad feng shui because it means that your luck can exit easily. A home is supposed to be the garden and the vault of your luck. This is what feng shui is for: to help you nurture and safeguard your luck. How many times have I walked into a potential town house and groaned at the sight of the staircase staring me in the face? Please, homebuilders, if you are reading this, please take notice. You are losing *so much money* by designing your properties this way.

We never did end up finding a house in Vancouver. In 2013, we moved to Toronto so I could cohost a new talk show. Jacek and I could only fly back and forth from Vancouver to Toronto so many times to look at homes. We found a real estate agent, narrowed down the neighborhood we wanted to live in, and gave her a list of requirements, the staircase issue being one of them. She emailed potential properties to us, and if we were in town, we'd check them out, after clearing the pictures with the Squawking Chicken so that she could tell us if it passed her preliminary dirt test.

But we weren't in town when the house we eventually bought came up for sale. It had a staircase issue. Normally, when a house had a staircase facing the door, we discarded it from the running immediately. This time, for some reason, Jacek ended up including it on a list of potentials that he emailed to my parents for review. Ma was all over it. She rang right away to say that this might be the one and that she wanted to make an appointment to go see it for us. We were shocked. *WTF? But what about the staircase?*

"Let me worry about that. I will go see it first."

She spent an hour and a half inside the house. And she loved it. She loved it so much she not only encouraged us to put in an offer, she approved of us going over asking. This is a woman who has a problem paying sales tax on groceries. The Squawking Chicken never goes over asking. That's how strongly she believed in this house.

And the staircase?

"Ma," Jacek asked, exasperated. "How come the staircase is okay?"

"When a house is strong, it can overcome its flaws. This house is strong. This house is very, very good for both of you." Feng shui—wind and water. If they are allowed to be, they can be flexible.

Our house is on the corner of a small intersection. The front door faces north, the back door faces south. So the sun comes in from three sides. That's a mega bonus—the house is light, there is very little room for shadows and darkness.

Because we're on the corner, the house sits on two streets. In feng shui terms, it means we have options—double the opportunity to maneuver, double the opportunity to escape, if necessary. That's a feature that's especially important for someone like me who works in a creative business. More roads lead to more imagination—the paths are open. Plus, in addition to a standard dining room, our kitchen has an island that can pass as an eating surface and it's been built with a breakfast nook. In Chinese, the slang expression for "making money" is "finding food." More places to "find food," i.e., eat, will give us more ways to make money.

We bought our house without ever stepping foot inside it, not even once. All that mattered was that it had the blessing of the Squawking Chicken.

Feng shui doesn't stop with the purchasing of a home. It's also how you arrange the furniture, the settings, the small details that seem insignificant but could be critical to how the home receives and grows your luck. For example, you should never set up your home so that you're facing a mirror as soon as you enter. Terrible luck. Mirrors are luck bouncers. You must be very careful where you position them. A mirror at the foot of the bed is also a problem. It will lead to marital strife and possible collapse. This is a feng shui basic. Another feng shui basic is that the foot of your bed should never face the bedroom door. Because that's how they wheel out a dead body—feet first. It'd be like sleeping in your coffin every night. There should also be no obstacles at the front of your house. Like a tree, or a lamppost. Those are luck blockers. How can luck come inside when it has to fight natural and man-made obstacles? Luck will just go next door, where it's easier to gain entry.

Basic feng shui principles for your home are now widely accessible online and at bookstores. But advanced feng shui is not so simple. This is what a feng shui master is for. Ma had a friend whose niece moved into a new house and suddenly became very sick. They discovered a tumor in her leg. After exhausting all medical options, they decided to bring in a feng shui master to assess the home. For the most part, the house was okay. The location was not a problem. There were no furniture placement issues. All the basics checked out. Turns out it was the fireplace. It was the source of all the problems. Something was up with the fireplace. The feng shui master recommended that the fireplace be sealed as soon as possible. He said that it was life-or-death. So they sealed the fireplace. Over eight weeks, her tumor started to shrink. The doctors were baffled but optimistic. They now had options for treatment. This happened as Christmas was approaching. The family was in good spirits. They wanted to have a festive Christmas after the stress of what they were going through. So they decided to unseal the fireplace, just for the holidays. It was a decision they would regret. In January her condition worsened. The cancer eventually metastasized to her lungs. She died that summer.

I will always remember Ma telling me afterward that no house is perfect. Every lucky house has an unlucky spot, and every unlucky house has a very lucky spot. We have yet to discover the lucky or unlucky spots in our new house. They will reveal themselves over time. What I can tell you, however, is that the Squawking Chicken will be there looking out for them. She has practically moved in. She is trying to make decisions on every furniture purchase and paint color and landscaping choice. She's even asserting herself about how we clean. The other day after sneezing a few times she was getting on me about how our air ducts need to be suctioned. Guess what happened when I protested?

Feng Shui Blackmail, of course.

"You think luck wants to come to a house that's dusty and messy? You think luck wants to hang out with you in your slum? You don't think luck has other options?" There's your incentive to keep your place tidy and not to clutter the entranceway.

It might sound restrictive, all these feng shui and fortune-telling requirements. I have friends who roll their eyes about what I can and cannot do, and when I should and shouldn't do it. A couple of years ago, the almanac predicted that Jacek, who was born under the sign of the Rabbit, could encounter some risk in a Rabbit-unfriendly year. The Squawking Chicken gave him a red string with a charm in the shape of a dog tied to the end of it and instructed him to keep it in the car. One of his buddies teased him about how it looked. Jacek, being the seasoned feng shui believer that he now is, laughed it off and kept it there anyway. At best it's a minor embarrassment to have to hang a cutesy animal charm from your wallet, or around your neck, or in your vehicle, or to scramble to find a papaya to eat before a live television event. At worst it's a slight inconvenience to have your blood taken, or seal a fireplace, or not hang that painting from that wall so that your friends will be impressed by your taste. But the Squawking Chicken would ask you if it's worth it.

Is it worth looking pretty at a party with your new bangs if it means you might not get that promotion? Is it worth having a show-off kitchen in a house that might threaten your marriage? For Ma, feng shui and fortune-telling advice is never such a hindrance that it becomes a difficult choice. You can't buy good luck with a million dollars, but bad luck might cost you that much. If eating a papaya every day might help me avoid that, why would I not eat the papaya?

When Ma was in the hospital battling POEMS, I asked her once whether or not she thought her life would have been different if she'd started practicing feng shui earlier. If she'd had someone to tell her about the hot water, the eye drops and the papayas, if she'd had someone giving her feng shui fortune-telling tips, would she have been betrayed so many times? Would she have been so often disappointed? Would she have had to endure so much sadness? In comparison, by the grace of her feng shui wisdom, I've had it so easy.

"You were born an Ox," Ma said. "You will never have it easy. An Ox is born to work and work hard. I'm just trying to help you work harder without distractions. Your life path as an Ox will be steady, so long as you can work. But I am a Tiger. The Tiger's life path is not steady. It is the Tiger's destiny to rise high, higher than anyone else. Over and over again. But with every high there is a fall. And a Tiger's falls go lower than most. That is the risk and the reward of being a Tiger. Feng shui and fortune-telling ensure that my highs last longer than my lows. But it can never eliminate the lows."

Ma was in bad shape at the time, a shriveled wretch in her hospital bed. It was hard to imagine that any high would be worth this low and all her previous lows. I pointed this out to her.

"CHOY!"

Even in her condition, the Squawking Chicken could still squawk when she had to. *Choy* is a Cantonese expression. It's spitting without actually spitting. It's a reaction to something blasphemous. Ma used to shout it in my face at dinner if I said I hated the food. *Choy! Don't let the fates hear you say you don't want the food. They might take it away.*

"Well, *look* at you," I said to Ma. "You're wearing a diaper. You look like a corpse. Your life sucks right now. Your life has sucked over and over again. Where is the high that can balance out those lows?"

She rolled her eyes in disgust, not unlike all those times I'd cut bangs. "What the hell do you think you are? Every Tiger has a roar. You are my roar. Now don't be so stupid. Otherwise you are just wasting my roar."

CHAPTER 8

Why Are You Dating a Triangle-Head?

The Squawking Chicken is terrible with names when meeting new people. Any names. Chinese names, English names, it doesn't matter, she barely remembers. Or she barely bothers to remember, I'm still not sure I know which. So instead of calling people by their actual names, she gives them Chinese nicknames, usually based on their physical attributes. This is her gift. She's able to identify exactly the characteristic that defines a person and then just applies this label to them for life.

Her dentist's assistant with the long eyelashes is Feather Face, because it always looks like there are two fans coming down from her forehead whenever she blinks. The man who lives two doors down with the paunch is Food Stealer because that's probably where he hoards it. My friend Margot is tall. She's simply Tall Girl. My other friend Kate is Flame

Top. She has red hair. Ma's nicknames are always a good indication of whether or not she likes a person. This was especially true when she started meeting my boyfriends.

I met Alan in college. We were friends for a while before we started dating. When we first met, I wasn't attracted to him at all. There were other guys in my life. There were other interests. Over time, however, we ended up hanging out more frequently. And the more time we spent together, Alan told me that he wanted to take our relationship to the next level. He confessed that he'd always been into me, and, well, I guess I was flattered. Transitioning from friendship to romance with Alan felt comfortable and easy, with no drama.

Alan was a good student. He also maintained a job at the same time. So he had his own car, his own money, and he was responsible and motivated. He came from a nice family. His parents were reasonably well-off, kind and generous. They were fond of me. They were supportive of our relationship. I'm telling you this because you'd think this would be a good enough résumé to bring home to your mother.

The Squawking Chicken met Alan for the first time when he dropped me off at home for a holiday long weekend. I invited him inside to say hello. Alan was a self-conscious person, rather particular about his appearance. He spent a lot of time tucking his T-shirts in just so. He wore boots under his jeans and made sure the pant legs were even on both sides. I used to tease him that he was so fastidious he'd even practice standing in front of the mirror, checking which side looked better when he leaned. Two hours later, I'd see him doing the preferred lean when we'd be out somewhere. The preferred lean came out for the Squawking Chicken. He was totally posing, there in the foyer, in a leather jacket and jeans, legs slightly spread apart, favoring one side, hands in his pockets. On the surface she was neither impressed nor unimpressed. It was a short, unremarkable conversation. She wasn't rude but she made no attempt to prolong it. Picking up on her cues, I motioned to Alan that it was time to go. When I came back inside after walking him to the car, I asked her what she thought of him.

"Why are you dating a Triangle-Head?"

Alan wasn't exactly George Clooney in the hair department, it's true. But he did the best he could. There was no comb-over situation or anything, but he did style it so that the thickest parts gathered near the front, peaking into a point above the middle of his forehead. It was fine, it wasn't a thing at all. At least not to me. The Squawking Chicken, however, decided that Alan was a pirate. His triangle of hair made it look like he was wearing a pirate's hat. So she insisted on calling him Triangle-Head, adding often that if he'd had an earring, he'd be perfect for the part. And from then on, during our yearlong relationship, she'd refer to him exclusively as Triangle-Head. We'd be at a family dinner and I'd leave at the end to go out with him and, as I was putting on my shoes, she'd tell everyone, loudly enough for me to hear, that "Elaine is going out with that Triangle-Head again, guard your ships!"

Finally, I confronted her. As I was getting ready to go out with Alan one night, I overheard Ma saying to Dad, "That Triangle-Head is coming to pick her up later." It just didn't make sense. In the past she'd criticized my boyfriends for being losers, for not having a "future," for lacking potential, for being lazy, for partying too much, for being perverted. (That last one was John—for the record, John was not a pervert. He just had a really sexy smile and it worked for him a lot of the time. John was a stud. And the Squawking Chicken could smell it on him right away. Because he knew how to work it on the girls.)

Alan was none of these things. Alan had a job. Alan was working toward a career in architecture. Alan had friends and an active social life but he wasn't excessive about hitting the club scene. And Alan definitely wasn't a pervert. So I asked Ma why she kept shitting on him. So he didn't have great hair, whatever. Was that the only thing she could hold against him?

"Your Triangle-Head is self-centered. I can tell by the way he stands. He stands like a pirate pretending to be a cowboy. Too much ego. He's not for you. You'll see."

The Squawking Chicken was trying to tell me that Alan was a poser. That he was too busy trying to be something else, he didn't know what he really was. (Who does, at twenty?) She had no time for him. And Alan had no time for her either. He knew that Ma wasn't warming to him; perhaps he sensed that she could *see* him. Rather than trying to change her mind, he shrugged it off. And occasionally he'd drop a subtle hint that it was her problem and not his. I could hear Ma's voice in my head whenever he'd behave this way. *If he's too proud to respect your parents, how much does he respect you?*

Alan and I lasted a year. He didn't want it to end, but eventually I just didn't want to spend time with him anymore. Where once his vanity was quirky, it later became a turnoff. Where once his posing and contrivances were cute, they soon became embarrassing. I can't say for sure whether or not I stopped wanting to be with him because I didn't want to be with him or because Ma didn't want me to be with him. Although she'd probably take credit, as she always does, for my eventual realization that Alan was, indeed, not for me, she wasn't exactly relieved when she found out we'd broken up. Instead, she seemed to *still* be irritated: "I don't understand how you could stay with a Triangle-Head for so long."

Looking back . . . me either. It's not like Alan was horrible or anything. He wasn't mean, he wasn't neglectful, I have no reason to resent him. But I also don't have a reason to remember him. He had an okay sense of humor, but he wasn't exceptionally funny. He was nice, but not extraordinarily kind. He was smart enough, but not exactly a genius. He was interesting enough, but I'd never say he was charismatic. And, well, as bitchy as this sounds, I wasn't even all that attracted to him. The Squawking Chicken was right. It was a whole year wasted—and on a relationship that I can't actually defend, a relationship that I never really wanted to fight for, a boyfriend I wish I could erase from my dating résumé so that I could have that time back and spend it with someone more sensitive or intelligent or creative or even someone hotter. Someone who's more than just a shrug in my memories. Someone I wouldn't be embarrassed to admit to having been with.

Ma tried to warn me early on about this. As soon as I started developing feelings for boys, she tried to warn me about how those feelings would look to the rest of the world. From the very beginning of my romantic journey, she cautioned me to be more discriminating about whom I chose to love.

My first love was Thomas. Thomas is the oldest son of my godmother, Mrs. Lai. (I call her "Auntie" Lai.) Thomas is five years older than his younger brother, Peter, who is a year older than I am. When we were younger, like any little sister, I was Peter's main target and he was always looking for ways to make fun of me. I was thirteen when I fell in love with Thomas. He was nineteen. He'd just graduated from high school. He was allowed to drive. He had a perm. He was beautiful. And he had a really pretty girlfriend so I kept my crush to myself. But in my daydreams, I imagined that Thomas and I would one day end up together. How could we not? Our families were so close. And he just needed to see me as a woman, which would happen as soon as my hair grew past my shoulders. I expected it to be long enough by the end of the summer, before I went back to Canada to begin the school year.

It was a weekend in July. Thomas's parents were hosting a barbecue at their place. I jealously watched Thomas and his girlfriend all night. One minute he was teasing her, the next minute he was feeding her sausages. It was infuriating. I was in a terrible mood. Ma was even worse. She and my stepfather had gotten into a fight about something and decided to go home. I had to leave with them. When we got back to our house, it went nuclear. Ma was screaming, my stepfather was pleading and I was sulking downstairs because I couldn't spy on Thomas anymore. Then I heard Ma dragging out her suitcases and yelling at me to start packing. She was threatening to leave. She called her friend Alice, the travel agent, to book a flight back to Canada.

I panicked. If we left, Thomas would never fall for me. Ma was killing my epic romance. Without thinking, I took off on my bike. I peddled frantically back to Thomas's house. It had cleared out by then. Thomas was in the yard, having just come back from seeing his girlfriend off at the bus stop. He smiled at me. That was my sign. I declared myself.

"Thomas, I have to go. I don't know when I'll be back, if ever. And I want you to know that I love you. And that one day we will be together."

Thomas was very kind. He gently let me down. He told me I was too young for him but that one day I would make someone very happy. What I heard was *one day you will make me very happy*. I rode home, daydreaming about our future life together, scheming about how I could convince Auntie Lai to adopt me. Ma and my stepfather had resolved their argument by the time I got back. Auntie Lai had invited them over for *siu yeh,* a midnight snack, common in our culture, especially on weekends. I was going to see Thomas again!

Peter started laughing as soon as we walked in the door. His mother shouted at him to stop it, but she was giggling too. And Uncle Lai. And Sandra, Peter and Thomas's sister. Everyone was laughing except for Thomas. At first I was confused. But I quickly realized that Thomas was smiling at me . . . pityingly. And then that I was the joke. Because Peter, that fucker, had overheard my profession of love. And, of course, he had to broadcast it to the world. He'd just finished broadcasting it to his own family, now he was about to broadcast it to mine. It was mortifying. And it was about to get worse.

Ma was overcome. She doubled over. She wept, she thought it was so funny. God, I was so mad. And I was terrified. Because by now I knew what she would do. I knew it would never end for me. I knew that instead of being Thomas's girlfriend, by the end of the summer I would be the Squawking Chicken's favorite joke. She joked about it the next day at mah-jong. She joked about it at Grandmother's. She joked about it until I got on the plane back to Canada. She joked about it even though I begged her, desperately, not to talk about it anymore. I begged her to stop embarrassing me. I begged her to stop telling everyone about how I threw myself at Thomas without thinking through my feelings.

"Oh, is that what you did?"

It is, indeed, what I did.

"Well, the next time you decide to do something like that, you better make sure you're okay with the world knowing about it. And if you're not, that's your problem, not mine."

In hindsight, I don't mind that everyone knew about my overwrought adolescent crush on Thomas. In that case, I have age as an excuse for my misguided ardor; naiveté was to blame for my angsty lack of awareness. But what's my excuse for Alan? What's my excuse for all the others?

We all have relationships we regret. Most of us rationalize that regret as a learning experience. Most of us understand that those learning experiences help us avoid future regret. The Squawking Chicken's perspective on regret and relationships, specifically *my* relationships, is not so generous. The way she sees it, if it looks like poison to begin with, why would you need to swallow it just to see if it's really poison? Because by the time you swallow it, it might be too late. Some poisonous relationships leave more than simple regret; they will alter your course forever. Where my love life was concerned, she made herself the human hazard sign on the bottle—a romantic roadblock determined to redirect my heart in the right direction using every resource at her disposal.

When I was fifteen, I met an older boy, Kwun, who lived in our Hong Kong neighborhood. My friend Candy had been hanging out with a crew of kids and she introduced me to Kwun when I came back for the summer holiday. He was a bad boy. I was instantly attracted. One night he wanted to go to the movies alone. So I told Ma that I was meeting up with Candy and took off on my bike. Instead Kwun and I held hands in the theater and kissed. When I came home that night, on time, she asked me where I'd been. The movies. *Who were you with?* Candy. Even when the words were coming out of my mouth, I knew that she knew—and I knew I was fucked.

The Squawking Chicken didn't just have a feeling that I wasn't being honest—she backed up that feeling by having me followed. Like I said, Ma grew up around local gangsters and law enforcement. She had contacts everywhere and they didn't mind spying for her when she asked them to. So the Squawking Chicken actually dropped a James Bond on my ass and uncovered my illicit teen romance. I wasn't allowed to see Kwun ever again.

I was young enough with Kwun that Ma could control the outcome of that situation. As I became more independent, though, she could only interfere so much. Still, she kept throwing herself in my path, sometimes literally. And I kept crashing through her barriers. If Kwun was a close call and Alan just a fender bender, Bobby was a major collision.

Bobby and I also started out as friends in college. When our relationship developed into something more, we decided not to attach any labels to what was between us. I'd recently broken up with Alan, Bobby had come out of a dramatic long-term relationship and we both wanted to keep it casual, not get too emotionally involved. Besides, I was graduating soon. It was my last year in college. I had no interest in attaching myself to someone for the summer and definitely not a guy who was going back to school in September. For weeks Bobby and I fronted like it would be realistic to just hang out all the time, for several nights at a time, and not engage on a deeper level. On a few occasions we even tried to not be together, just to prove that we could, as if by simply not being in the same room it would mean that we weren't wanting to be in the same room. Obviously we were in love. And it was a lot of fun. At the beginning, there was an intensity to what we had that was exciting and fresh. I had finished my fourth year. I was the first in my family, on either side, to complete a post-secondary education. My parents were very proud. As I was their only child, they knew they only had one chance. And I had delivered. Now it was summer and I was free. Bobby and I were inseparable, except that before we hooked up, I had planned a trip to Los Angeles to see a friend and now I found that I didn't want to leave him.

I went on the trip. I was supposed to be in L.A. for a week. After five days, I decided to change my ticket and go home. Bobby's parents were away and he had the house to himself. My plan was to come back to Toronto two days early, spend the weekend with him and then go back to my parents' and they wouldn't know the difference. Bobby came to pick me up at the airport. I was devious too. I called often. I blocked the number before dialing. I thought I had totally convinced her that I was still in L.A. But that sixth sense of hers kicked in again.

Ma somehow knew that I was messing around behind her back with Bobby the same way she knew that I was sneaking around with Kwun—it's more than just mother's intuition, it's a sick gift. Bobby and I had enjoyed a full day of pure awesome before the phone rang. I was watching TV when he came back into the living room and told me it was the Squawking Chicken on the line. I was terrified. But by then I was so in love with Bobby and so unwilling to be apart from him, I was determined not to go home yet. So I braced myself for that voice. I readied myself for her wrath. Instead, she was dead-voiced. "Are you safe?" was all she asked.

So it was the guilt play. And I immediately understood how worried she must have been when she couldn't find me in L.A. I had disappeared without telling anyone where I was going. It was horribly irresponsible. In that moment, I recognized that it was selfish, and that I was too absorbed in my own passion to think about Ma's feelings. But still, un-like how it was with Kwun so many years before, this time I had the will to defy her. Or I should say by this point I was so hopelessly in love with Bobby, it superseded everything else, even the Squawking Chicken's hold over me. It was the first time in my life that I had rebelled against her and so flagrantly. I stayed with him for the full two days.

When I finally returned home that evening, reluctantly, and not because I didn't want to face her but because I didn't want to leave Bobby, Ma shrugged like she'd barely noticed I was gone. At that point, she had other preoccupations. Ma was diagnosed with Berger's disease the year before I started dating Bobby. Berger's disease affects the kidneys. Both of Ma's kidneys had stopped functioning and she was self-administering peritoneal dialysis at home every day. She was constantly in and out of the hospital with infections and other medical emergencies. The Squawking Chicken was facing a health crisis and I was so consumed by Bobby, I completely checked out. Dad hadn't yet retired then so she was alone while he spent the day at the office, and she was alone again in the evenings after Dad had gone to bed so that he could wake up in the morning to go to work. They were sleeping in separate bedrooms at this point because Ma was restless through the night.

She was sick and afraid. And she was alone. Just as so many family members and loved ones had abandoned her before, her daughter was abandoning her too. I was totally useless. All I cared about that summer was being with Bobby. So many nights I was torn, seeing her in her bedroom, attached to a machine that was stepping in where her organs had failed, her face a worried, lonely gray, and still I'd find the coldness in my heart to open the door, close it, lock it behind me and get into Bobby's car. By the time he pulled out of the driveway, I'd have forgotten the ache of remorse in my soul for leaving her behind, replaced by the warmth of his hand in mine, and we were off, selfish, indulgent lovers until dawn.

Ma did not interfere with Bobby and me for the rest of the summer. She knew it had to end. Bobby had one more year left in college and I had to start looking for a job. Or, rather, I was expected to start looking for a job. Ma may have resigned herself to the reality of my relationship but she wasn't about to financially support it. I found a placement at a small insurance firm shortly after he left to go back to school. The days were boring and excruciatingly long. Bobby and I saw each other on weekends but he had a real life on campus. My life existed only from Friday to Sunday when we were together. After a couple of months of long distance, I couldn't bear it anymore. One weekend, while visiting him at school, I decided I just wouldn't go back to work. Since I wasn't spending anything during the weekdays when we weren't together, I had saved enough to be able to coast for a few weeks without a job, living with him in his apartment on campus. It was enough to last me to the holidays, and then I figured I'd just start working again in January.

Ma simply didn't have the strength to protest. And Dad didn't want to further upset her by confronting me. Besides, he was only focused on getting her better. The peritoneal dialysis wasn't working as well as the doctors had hoped and they were now planning to switch her over to hemodialysis. This would require surgically creating a fistula on her left arm to allow her blood to pass through a machine that would essentially act as a kidney. Without her opposition, I happily spent my days lazing around Bobby's apartment, slowly losing my identity.

Then it was Christmastime. Bobby went home and so did I. Ma's condition had stabilized and she was gaining strength in preparation for the fistula surgery in the new year. I took advantage of her brief improvement and convinced myself she was better than she was so that I could spend even more time with Bobby, accepting every invitation to his family gatherings. And when January came around, despite the fact that I was out of money, I got back into his car and returned to campus with him. Six weeks passed—time evaporates in a love haze, and suddenly it was February, almost an entire year since I'd taken my last college exam, and still I was doing nothing with my life.

Bobby and I were back in Toronto for spring break. He wanted to go snowboarding. But I was broke and Ma wasn't funding me. I was so desperate to not miss even one day with him that I hit up a pawnshop and sold the twenty-four-karat gold necklace that she'd given me to raise the cash I needed to be able to keep clinging to Bobby. The Squawking Chicken busted me pretty quickly for that one too. Again, her weird telepathy where I was concerned kicked in. And when I came home from the ski trip to drop off my clothes and pick up a few things before heading back out again, with Bobby, of course, she looked for it right away— for the necklace that was no longer hanging around my neck. She knew what I had done without me having to tell her. The Squawking Chicken had had it. She'd quietly watched me piss myself away for six months and she finally decided it was time to shout.

I could feel it coming. So I ran upstairs to quickly get what I needed before escaping, thinking I could make it back down and out the door without too much drama. By the time I reached the bottom step, though, she'd already found the time to stomp to the kitchen, grab a knife and park herself in the foyer, blocking my exit.

There she was, the Squawking Chicken, in a nightgown, her hair in disarray, her voice as loud as ever, ringing off every wall of the house, her eyes wild, and, frankly, more alive than they'd been in a long time, holding a knife to her throat as Dad stood beside her futilely pleading with her to calm the fuck down.

"If you leave again and go with that boy, I will die in your face, I will die in your face, I will die in your face!"

It was a killer performance. Even at the time, I remember thinking to myself, seriously, that she was throwing down an Oscar-worthy piece of acting. This was the ultimate guilt trip, the guilt trip of all time, the Super Bowl of all guilt trips. How many mothers have the balls to threaten to commit suicide because they hate your boyfriend? I remember grudgingly admiring her move.

There was no way she was going to off herself in front of me . . . right? Probably not. But then again, I had spent my entire life watching Ma's strategic unpredictability. The element of doubt was enough. This was her trump card in a battle of wills. The Squawking Chicken had just been waiting for the right time to play it.

Ma won the hand and I stayed home. Later that night, when the situation had calmed down, she came to speak to me. I was sulking and I was bitter, but mostly I was stressed about not being with Bobby. I was worried that he was having a good time without me, and that he'd want to have more good times without me. She could feel my anxiety and she understood exactly where it was coming from.

"He won't love you for very long, you know? He won't love you because right now, you're not worth loving."

The Squawking Chicken was telling me that I was a loser. And I was. But I wasn't ready to admit it to myself yet. I was too stubborn to acknowledge that Ma might have been right. And besides, to me, back then, I didn't exactly see her as a boss in how she had handled her own relationships. If I was a loser, I was only learning from the best. After all, in the fucked-up love life department, she was a total rock star.

Ma had left Dad all those years ago because he was too immature to stand up to his family's mistreatment of her. So she ended up with Uncle, who promised her security and loyalty but ended up cheating on her. Uncle was weak, sure, and showed a lack of character, obviously, but still, at the same time, he never had a chance. Because Uncle wasn't Dad, and through it all, Ma has always been in love with Dad. He knew she had promised Dad that if he made something of himself that she would return. And wasn't it convenient that just as Dad made good on his part, Uncle screwed up? Uncle had given Ma a way out.

I was six years old when my parents broke up. I was there at the precise moment when they split. I was sixteen years old when they started the process of getting back together. I was there at the precise moment that they reunited. Literally.

Ma had come back to Canada after Uncle's infidelity, telling him that she needed some time to consider her options. Dad and I were planning a four-day road trip with Sally and Don, his business partners, and their son, Scott. Ma decided to join us. We were going to New York but staying in New Jersey because the hotels are cheaper there. And the Squawking Chicken wanted to gamble in Atlantic City.

Each family had their own hotel room with two queen-size beds. I slept in one bed with Ma, Dad slept in the other. In the middle of the night, on the final night of the holiday, I woke up because I heard noises.

There was bed creaking.

There was heavy breathing.

There was flesh connecting.

MY PARENTS WERE DOING IT TWO FEET AWAY FROM ME.

You are crazy if you think I stayed there, suffering silently, until it was over. No. The minute I realized that they were having sex TWO FEET AWAY FROM ME, I screamed, jumped out of bed, and locked myself in the bathroom. It was chaos after that. Dad started pounding on the door, begging me to open it, apologizing over and over again. I shouted at them that I hated them and never wanted to speak to them again. Typical teenage threats. Then Dad started moaning, "We've ruined her forever! We've ruined her life forever!"

And the Squawking Chicken? For her it was just a regular evening. Like it happens all the time that a girl would find herself in a goddamn motel room in New Jersey sleeping next to her fucking parents actually fucking.

She waited out my hysteria. She talked Dad off the ledge. Then she calmly and authoritatively reminded me that we had to wake up early the next morning so don't come to bed too late. And that was it. One day I had a stepfather in Hong Kong. The next my parents were living together again. After living for ten years as a child of divorce, I was now, at sixteen, expected to acclimate to being part of a "whole" family without justification or input.

Seven years later, deeply mired in my own romantic entanglements, I called the Squawking Chicken out on her own relationship bullshit. I might have been throwing it all away for Bobby, but it's not like she was qualified to judge me.

Not surprisingly, Ma was unrepentant.

"If you think I made mistakes, why aren't you trying to be better? At least I have an excuse for my mess. I came from nothing. I had nothing to offer. You have so much to offer and you still found a way to make yourself into nothing. Bobby's not going to stay for someone who's nothing."

And he didn't. Unlike me, he had plans after college. He'd been accepted into an overseas teaching program. The sad fool that I was, I intended to follow him there too. We decided that he would go first and I would join him a month later. Two weeks before he left, though, after a long discussion with his mother, he told me he was going alone. Is that irony?

Bobby's mother was proud of her son. He had a degree. He had opportunities. He had a placement with a well-respected educational exchange program that would improve his skill set in a foreign country. He had a girlfriend who'd been dicking around for an entire year and had to sell off jewelry just to go snowboarding. So she asked him—did he really want to start this new chapter in his life with a person who was less-than?

I was officially less-than.

And I was judged to be less-than, not by my own mother, but by someone else's. It's the shame that endures, you know? The shame lasts so much longer than the heartbreak. This is why the Squawking Chicken spent so much time shaming me at home. Shaming me by barbecue pork. Shaming me in public. Shaming me with love in the hope that I would avoid being shamed by strangers, by mothers of boyfriends for whom I wasn't good enough. The same way she was shamed by her husband's family who tried to make her feel like she wasn't good enough.

I realized then that the tragedy wasn't Bobby leaving me. The deepest cut was that my experience with Bobby led me to realize the Squawking Chicken's greatest fear: I had become her. And worse still, I didn't have to. Ma gave me every opportunity to avoid being powerless so that I would never be at the mercy of a man. And I had voluntarily put myself at the mercy of a man the way she seemed to always find herself at the mercy of them. This force of a woman, with the most indomitable spirit I have ever known, a phoenix seemingly undefeatable, didn't want me to be like her at all.

Nothing is more humbling than to know your mother's darkest truth. The Squawking Chicken's darkest truth was that her wanting me to be more-than was based on her belief that she was the one who was less-than. It's up to me to prove that she isn't. That started by loving smarter. For both of us.

∂ᢙ

Two days after we met briefly at work and well before we'd even had our first conversation, Jacek went home and told his mother about me. Right from the start, I was never less-than for Jacek. Which is why he's never been less-than for the Squawking Chicken.

He doesn't flinch when she sticks her hand out and asks for money. He has submitted to every baffling feng shui fortune-telling requirement even when he doesn't understand it. In 2008 we visited my parents in Hong Kong for

Christmas. One day before we left to go sightseeing on our own, Ma wanted me to bring a sweater. It was warm, I didn't want to carry it around. Jacek had a small messenger bag with him, but he didn't want to carry it around either. She suggested that he was lazy, and that made him a bad husband because he would rather risk me catching cold than be inconvenienced. Understandably, he was annoyed. But he didn't take it personally and he didn't challenge her either. Instead, he defused the situation by laughing it off, tucking the sweater into the bag, and teasing her to change the mood. By these small gestures and his good-natured submission, he was passing her tests.

Jacek has had to endure many of Ma's tests. He passed his first test when he was invited to come over to the house. Ma's doctors were monitoring her kidney function at the time. They needed to evaluate her urine over a period of twenty-four hours, so she'd been urinating into a jug that she kept in a cupboard above the bathroom sink. Dad was busy doing something else and couldn't reach up and get it for her. From the kitchen, I heard her ask MY NEW BOY-FRIEND:

"Jacek, can you help me to do my twenty-four-hour pee-pee?"

I didn't panic. I didn't rush over with a million excuses. I didn't worry that he'd break up with the girl whose mother walked around telling perfect strangers to handle her pee-jug. But I was impressed with the guy who handled Ma's pee-jug, no problem. And so was the Squawking Chicken. Sure, it was an unorthodox request. But his desire to be helpful trumped his discomfort. He wasn't embarrassed by the request because he wasn't thinking about himself. He was just thinking that this woman was obviously sick and needed his assistance. Jacek proved that he is not driven by ego. His natural reaction to her twenty-four-hour pee-pee showed he is self-assured enough to not let ego damage relationships. That he is mature enough to not be petty. That he is strong enough in his own self to know that being with a strong woman doesn't make him less of a man, but in actuality, even more of a man. And also that he has empathy. He was able to fill in the blanks, give her the benefit of the doubt that she wouldn't be asking him to help her with her twenty-four-hour pee-pee if not for her ongoing health issues.

Jacek was there for her when she was hospitalized before her POEMS syndrome diagnosis, shriveled to ninety-five pounds, scared and hurting, and struggling to communicate in English with a medical team that couldn't figure out what was killing her. I had a work commitment and had to travel.

Ma was insistent that I not jeopardize my career because of her health problems. So it was Jacek who flew from Vancouver to Toronto to spend a week at her bedside, taking the day shift so Dad could sleep and spend the nights there, setting up his workstation in the corner of the room, lifting the straw to her mouth when she was thirsty, discussing with the doctors their next course of treatment, buoying her spirits when she became despondent, distracting her by asking her to tell him her history. With her life in the balance, the Squawking Chicken had a son to support her and stand up for her. Jacek is the husband to me that she had waited thirty years for Dad to be for her.

Is it a great love story or a sad love story that the Squawking Chicken only experienced marital satisfaction when she was facing possible death? Dad had disappointed Ma in his youth. He was incapable of defending her and their partnership in the face of family conflicts. In overcoming his own insecurities, however, he tried to demonstrate to her that they could confront obstacles together, united. He pledged to her that it would be different when she came back to him. Even still, given her grudging nature, and conditioned by a lifetime of emotional treachery, she struggled with forgiveness. Before her illness, every time Dad was in a funk, every time they got into an argument, she'd dredge up the past, she'd list all his inadequacies, she'd recount, over and over again, the incidents when he'd let her down, the occasions when he didn't have her back. Ma's inability to Get Over It became as detrimental to their love as Dad's past shortcomings.

Ma was waiting for her warrior. And just as she thought her life was over, he came. Dad was single for ten years after Ma left him. There were colleagues at work who tried to set him up. He once went on a few dinner dates with a woman who was interested in more. Ma told me later that when the woman pressed, Dad couldn't do it. I was his priority. And he was waiting. Dad was waiting for the Squawking Chicken to come back. Every night he'd study until two or three o'clock in the morning, then he'd get up to drive me to school and he'd take on as many jobs as he could. On the days he felt tired and wanted to give up, he'd think of his motivation: Ma had promised she'd come back when he deserved her. Ma was his motivation. Ma has always been his *only* motivation. It's not that Dad loves me less than he loves her, but Dad's life—his happiness, his dreams—has never been dependent on mine. He understands and accepts that I will find my own fulfillment separate from him. His fulfillment, however, is inextricably linked to her.

In her sickness, Dad found his redemption. Morning to night he was there with her in the hospital. We've never seen a more devoted husband, the nurses would say. He changed her diapers. He cleaned up the vomit. A small person himself, he carried her in his arms up and down the halls because it was too painful for her to sit in a wheelchair, her bones bumping up against the steel. I saw the determination in his face, even as his thin arms trembled from muscle spasms and his legs wobbled from the weight. *Let me do this for you now,* he was saying. *Let every step be an apology for every time I let you down before.* As he cradled her they would dream together, making plans for after recovery.

When you get better, we'll go here . . .

When you can walk again, we'll do this . . .

Will I ever walk again? she asked.

You have to walk again, he'd answer. *You are the only thing I have. You are the only thing I have ever had.*

And this is my father's darkest truth: he may not have always known how to keep her, but the Squawking Chicken is all he's ever wanted.

Ma finally felt wanted.

CHAPTER 9

That's So Low Classy

There was a girl I had a crush on in my first year in college. Not in a romantic way, but in the platonic way that girls crush on other girls: we want to dress like them, we want to move like them, act like them, have friends like they have, *be* them. I called her Annabelle, because Annabelle was my favorite name then—and she looked like an Annabelle: effortlessly confident, comfortable in any environment, a person people seemed to gravitate to.

The first time I saw my girl crush was at the D. B. Weldon Library at the University of Western Ontario. It was the first month of school, when I was still motivated to go to class and do my readings, not so much because I was dedicated to my studies, but because it was fun to play the part of "college student." Being at the library seemed like a scene

from a movie—during the montage, when the main character, a Winona Ryder type, could be found perusing Jane
Austen, as Shanice's "I Love Your Smile" played in the background.

But pretending your life is a rom-com movie montage
gets old really quickly. I had just started to get bored with
pretending to be learning when I looked up and there she
was, my new obsession, the girl who should have been the
Winona Ryder character in my movie montage, striding
toward my table.

She had long, wavy brown hair—thick and rich, the exact
style I had always wanted to grow myself—creamy olive
skin; big, warm, green eyes; perfect teeth; a few freckles here
and there; and a very becoming summer tan, even though
the weather had just started to cool. Also, her clothes were
amazing: a thin tan sweater over khaki pants and riding
boots. She carried a leather backpack with her textbooks in
her arms, folded over her chest as two surfer boys followed
behind her. When I died, I decided, that was how I wanted
to come back to life.

It turns out that I was occupying her regular spot. She
wasn't a bitch about it though. Instead, my Annabelle was
friendly: "Oh hey, haven't seen you around here before. Are
you in first year?" Annabelle sat down. I felt like a loser.

Smiling meekly, I nodded and went back to not reading my French.

After a few minutes, it became too much; I knew if I stayed there, I'd eventually beg her to be my friend. So I packed up and left, preferring instead to creep on her without her knowing, which is what I did for the next few weeks. I think I even cut a few classes just to spy on her. It was never for long, my stalking. Ten minutes at a time, max. Just enough so that I could see who she was with—always a really fun party crowd (they went out a lot but they weren't total fuck-ups either)—and what she was doing and how she looked. She was perfect every single time. Until the one time that changed everything.

It was December. It was exam season. We were all a little harried and dry-skinned. Except, of course, for my Annabelle, who wore cute glasses and managed to stay moisturized. I was taking a break in the early evening at the food court at the university community center, facing the library. Light snow was falling outside and she came in, wearing a black wool coat, snow in her hair, her face flushed from the cold, like Ali MacGraw in *Love Story*. I was *so* happy I'd decided to be hungry at exactly the right time.

She was with a few friends. They ordered and sat down at a table across the hall where, facing forward, I could see the side of her body. She was seated closest to me. And that's when it happened. That's when I saw her doing it. She was doing the leg thing. As she ate, she bounced her leg up and down, jiggling it incessantly. My immaculate idol was leg twitching like the junkies Ma used to point out with disdain on the street in Yuen Long. I was *so* mad I had decided to be hungry at exactly the wrong time. It turns out Annabelle, my immaculate idol, was Low Classy.

Low Classy is the term the Squawking Chicken uses to describe coarse behavior. Leg jiggling is a coarse motion. There is no elegance in leg jiggling. There is no refinement. On the few occasions I jiggled my leg as a child, Ma would slap me on the thigh, stare me down with the death eyes, and scold me, loudly, of course: "That's so Low Classy. I don't care if you're the Queen, if you're jiggling your leg you may as well be a degenerate on the street corner."

Ma curtailed my leg jiggling early. And then I started judging the leg jigglers. Like Annabelle. After the leg-jiggling incident, Annabelle was dead to me. Leg jiggling has become a deal-breaker, not only for girl crushes but also for proper romantic crushes. I once ended a date midway through dinner because of leg jiggling. I used to be a big fan of a certain male movie star until he started leg jiggling during our interview. I have since stopped seeing his films. Due to the Squawking Chicken's classification of the Low Classiness of leg jiggling, it is as repellent to me as it is to her, although I'm much more subtle about my disdain. Annabelle never knew that I stopped caring about her. (Hopefully she never knew that I cared about her in the first place.) Ma, on the other hand, regularly goes around hissing at the people doing Low Classy things. Her top Low Classy moves include:

⊃⊆

Walking and Smoking at the Same Time

Ma smoked well into her late forties, until her kidneys started failing. But she only smoked when she was sitting down. It's ladylike and elegant to smoke in a seated position, to take time in between drags, indulging in the habit gracefully. Those who walked and smoked were hustlers, gangsters on the move, rolling from one crime to the next. Or a hooker rushing from one john to the other.

Ma also considers it Low Classy to talk with a cigarette hanging from your mouth. A well-bred person waits between inhales, and exhales before speaking instead of letting her words dangle from her lips along with the cigarette. My uncle's ex-wife, Heidi, used to speak with a cigarette between her teeth all the time at the mah-jong table. Heidi was a rough woman with a low voice who used to bartend at sketchy pubs in the worst parts of town. She was kind and meant well but she had the worst manners ever. Ma was always correcting her Low Classiness and whenever she started saying something with a smoke in her mouth, Ma would rag on her right away, sometimes even telling her that that's why her husband left her. Heidi just laughed. She was too entrenched in her habits to change. Though she and my uncle are no longer married, she and Ma have remained friends. In fact, the Squawking Chicken probably likes her more than she likes her own brother. Heidi's Low Classy talking and smoking was not a friendship deal-breaker. Some Low Classy behaviors can be balanced by character and Heidi has a good heart. Other Low Classy behaviors, however, are a direct result of major character flaws. And that kind of Low Classiness can never be forgiven.

Pouting

I've never been to France with the Squawking Chicken, but I've always wondered whether or not she'd spend the whole time in Paris yelling at people for being Low Classy. Then again, seeing as France is the land of the name brand, perhaps she'd be more forgiving. But French girls are famous for the pout. And according to the Squawking Chicken, pouting, or any kind of mouth twitch, like the "duck face" pictures people post of themselves on social media these days (pushing your lips together like you want to give someone the fattest, wettest kiss of all time), is super Low Classy. Mostly because, in Ma's mind, it suggests that the pouter is horny.

I used to pout a lot when I was a kid and through my teens. When I was in a shitty mood, when something didn't go my way, when a cute boy was around and I wanted to seem grown-up. But when you're sitting at the same table as a guy you're trying to impress, nothing kills a pout like being told that when you're pouting you look like a hooker ready to perform a blow job. I was fourteen when that happened. We were at a group dinner at the country club in Hong Kong with some mah-jong aunties and their families. One of the aunties, Mrs. Leung, had an older son, about twenty, who was home for summer holiday from England, where he went to college. David wore a smart pink shirt with the collar turned up and had his hair styled like George Michael. (It was the eighties. What do you want from me?) I was thrilled when we ended up sitting with the Leungs. Naturally I played it nonchalant and cool, not speaking much and feigning boredom during the entire meal, pouting in between bites like the models—Linda, Naomi, Christy!—who were plastered all over my bedroom, torn from the pages of *Vogue* and *Elle*. The Squawking Chicken was clearly not feeling my mysterious, woman-of-the-world vibe. Instead: "What's wrong with you? Why are you doing that with your mouth? I told you to stop doing that with your mouth. Only women who want to use their mouths on men do that with their mouths." Then, to everyone else: "I hate people who pout. That's so Low Classy."

I don't blush. It's a physiological impossibility for me. And I was grateful for this at that moment. As teenagers do, I claimed I wasn't feeling well instead so I was allowed to ride my bike home and contemplate suicide for the rest of the night. Needless to say, I avoided David the rest of that summer and never saw him again.

∂⑤

Leaning

Ma hates leaners as much as she hates pouters. One day Ma and I pulled up at a 7-Eleven for some snacks and there were some teenagers outside loitering. She started muttering about how Low Classy they were and how they must have shitty parents. I was around twelve at the time, fascinated by kids older than me, cooler than me. I didn't see the problem. She pointed out that half of them were leaning against the side of the store. This was lazy. Young people who couldn't stand up straight were lazy. The whole world could see that they were leaning and lazy and useless and therefore unproductive. People who are raised well, from good families, do not lean.

∂⑤

Wearing Wrinkled and/or Low-Cut Clothing

Ma irons everything, even towels. She puts a lot of effort into her attire, even if she's just going out for groceries. Her clothes are always pressed, always clean, never even a piece of lint. For the Squawking Chicken, it's all about presentation.

"People will judge you on your first appearance," she used to say to me before job interviews. She always judges on first appearances. Wrinkles are a disgrace. Wrinkles are Low Classy. The person who voluntarily walks around with wrinkles is the person who doesn't care about himself and as such can't be trusted. When Jacek met my parents for the first time, I was on his ass nonstop about wrinkles. If he showed up in wrinkles, I knew she'd hate him on sight. He ended up ironing his jeans and even his sweater.

I have since learned that different cultures have different comportment standards for Low Classy. Jacek's Polish father thinks it's Low Classy when a man stands around with his hands in his pockets. I don't necessarily agree, but I can see why it would offend old-school thinkers. Keeping your hands in your pockets isn't open or polite. It's like you're hiding something, not transparent. In other words, Low Classy.

Then again, you don't want to show too much. For the Squawking Chicken, too much is cleavage. Chinese women are pretty conservative in personal style compared to Westerners. Westerners are a lot more comfortable showing more skin. Ma believes that the way a woman dresses can indicate how loose, or not loose, she is. A woman in wrinkled clothing, obviously, spends too much time on her back to care about looking presentable. A woman who's presenting her breasts first obviously only cares about being on her back.

∂G

Being Affectionate in Public

PDA ranks high on the Squawking Chicken's list of Low Classy offenses. Kissing, hugging and even hand-holding should not be on display. Those who present their physical love to the world must have been bred in brothels. It is undignified. If that's what they're doing in public, imagine the crazy shit they must be doing in private.

Ma started hammering this into me early. A man would put his arm around his girlfriend in a movie theater and she'd spend the whole movie making snide comments about how disgusting it was that they were practically fucking in their seats. A woman would spoon a mouthful of rice into her husband's mouth at a restaurant and Ma would glare at them through the entire meal, accusing the lady of being easy, concluding that that was the only reason the guy was with her. We'd be waiting for the train on the platform and a young couple holding hands would kiss, lightly, not even making out, and she'd walk by them, muttering loud enough for them to hear her calling them tramps.

And it's not limited to the romantic either. As I mentioned earlier, she's not warm, the Squawking Chicken. She doesn't receive hugs well. This has made for some hilarious moments in North America, a rather huggy culture. When my friends came over and tried to hug her, she looked like they were handing her a used diaper. The first time my husband, Jacek, moved to hug her she looked like she wanted to slap him. Even when I hug her, and I have done so more and more as she's been in the hospital so much, she shrinks away, like I'm about to infect her with something, usually dog hair, which is what she almost always says as soon as I touch her.

"Don't get your dogs' hair all over me. It's so gross, all that dog hair you have all over yourself. That's so Low Classy." She means the hair *and* the hugging.

Indeed, the more tactile the person, the Low Classier she or he is. Combine that with verbal affection and you may as well be dead to her. As previously mentioned, the Squawking Chicken isn't great with corny talk. If we're watching a soap opera and two lovers are sharing their feelings, she'll start hollering to turn the channel or she'll get up in a huff and ruin the moment for those who are enjoying it. The verbal sweetness is sickening to her. Partly it's because she doesn't think words can ever properly capture sentiment. It just ends up feeling insincere, no matter how sincere the expression was intended to be. And also it's the way it sounds. Because our voices change when we're conveying emotion. You don't tell someone you care for them in the same way you order a coffee. You adjust the delivery, you soften the tone. Like . . . baby talk. The tone of love is baby talk. And it's the tone of love that Ma finds so repulsive, especially coming from a female. To her, it's simpering. Fake. Dishonest then. And therefore manipulative, the kind of womanly wile she considers the defining mark of a cheap Low Classy woman. A woman like Jane.

Jane was Ma's roommate at the hospital where she received her radiation treatments after her POEMS diagnosis. Jane arrived a few weeks after Ma had settled in. Jane was also Chinese, replacing Constance, an elderly white woman Ma greatly admired. Constance was tidy and kept to herself. She read a lot of books and had good posture. Constance occupied the bed by the window and when she was discharged, Ma took over that spot and waited to see who would be next. At first, she was happy about Jane's arrival because they spoke the same language. Jane said she was a retired schoolteacher, which impressed Ma, and they made plans to go for dim sum when they were both let out of the hospital. Ma liked Jane so much at the beginning she even asked her personal caregiver, Gloria, to help her get around. Every time I called her, she went on about Jane this and Jane that. She was all over Jane, in a good way. So when I came to visit, I began to make conversation with Ma's new friend, grateful to the person who was making her recovery more bearable. Until the Squawking Chicken abruptly barked at me to come over to her side, awkwardly ending the conversation. She was foul for a while after that. Finally, when Jane left the room, I asked her why she was in such a bad mood.

"I don't want you to have any more contact with that woman. She's Low Classy."

I looked over at Gloria, who just shrugged and walked

away. It was because Jane had visitors—three different men who came on different days. And when they'd come to see her, Jane would put on the baby talk. She had nicknames for each of them. Egg Tart was the dude who came on Mondays and Wednesdays. Piggy was the one who came on Tuesdays and Thursdays. The Chief visited on weekends. But she'd speak to all of them in the same way. Jane's love voice drifted over to Ma's side of the room like a diseased cloud. *Oh Eggy! Why are you so late today? Don't you know I've been waiting for you?*

Worse still was the fact that Jane would be fine before their arrival and then act like she'd been suffering as soon as they got there. *Thank God you're here, Piggy. I've had such a rough time lately. It's been so terrible. You must help me feel better.*

Ma made it sound like Jane was ripping off her clothes every time Egg Tart, Piggy or the Chief came around. She made a face like something was rotting, like Jane's baby talk was accompanied by a foul stench that hovered over their beds.

Ma was stuck. She was handicapped and she was being forced to listen to a woman moan and mewl, as she put it, in a man's face four days a week.

That's so Low Classy.

It was everything Ma hated in a woman: weak, phony and wanton.

And so the Squawking Chicken let it be known that she was offended. Whenever Egg Tart or Piggy came around, she'd have Gloria draw the privacy curtain right away, and with force, clearly dividing the room between the Low Classy side and the High Classy side. I showed up one day when Piggy was there and the curtain was drawn. Not knowing the symbolism behind the curtain, I tried to push it back because it made Ma's section feel cramped and dark. She stopped me right away. There was a gleam in her eye when I asked her why. I had played right into her plan. "I can no longer watch what's happening over there. In broad daylight! A woman with no shame bringing shame on me by association! Low Classy! Low Classy!"

She made it sound like it was porn. Like Jane and Piggy were triple X-ing each other by whispering sweet nothings. Later on, as I wheeled her down to the cafeteria, I suggested that maybe Jane was lonely, and if having three companions come visit her on the regular, sharing harmless words of affection, was helping her convalesce, maybe Ma could ease up on being such a bitch.

"I'd rather be lonely than Low Classy." And then: "Only home wreckers act like that, not caring who sees, who hears."

The home wrecker is the embodiment of all that is Low Classy.

Home Wrecking

I went on my first Home Wrecker Hunt when I was eleven years old. As usual, we were at Grandmother's mah-jong den, always where the action went down. Ma's table was waiting on the final player—Ah Jun (whose husband, by the way, was a leg jiggler). Ma thought he was shit because he treated Ah Jun like shit, even though she doted on him, scrambling off in the middle of a game whenever he called for his dinner, crying on her way back whenever he bailed, which was often, because he had a mistress.

Ah Jun was a mess when she showed up that afternoon. Her face was red, her hair was unwashed, but she refused to explain why when she sat down at the table. Everyone tried to ignore her at first. Even Ma was remarkably restrained. She would have continued to overlook her disheveled state but Ah Jun kept fucking up the cards. She'd be overdrawn on her deck and have to forfeit. Or she'd call the two of circles as her winning tile when she was actually waiting on the three of circles. In mah-jong, when you call a win for the wrong tile, you end up having to pay the other players a maximum hand amount as a penalty. Ma wasn't having any fun. That was the problem. Ah Jun was normally a decent competitor. This was a waste of Ma's time. Finally, Ma had had enough. She stopped the game and made Ah Jun tell her what was up.

Ah Jun's husband had spent the night over at his mistress's. That morning, after he left to go to work, the mistress called Ah Jun to lord it over her. "He's sleeping here now. He likes it better here, better than at home with you. Pretty soon, you'll never see him." The mistress was evidently rather descriptive, boasting about the carnal benefits of her place over Ah Jun's.

That's so Low Classy.

Ma was furious. Nothing was Low Classier than a flagrant home wrecker. A proper home wrecker knew her place and hid her face, shamed by her home wrecking. A home wrecker had no business making contact with the wife, who was official, who had social standing, who lived in the light.

This Low Classy home wrecker had to be told.

Ma threw down her chips. She ordered the mah-jong stopped at all the other tables as well. Then, the Squawking Chicken, in her signature screech, rallied her troops. She was a general leading her forces into battle. She was fighting the Low Classy. "Ah Jun has been disrespected by a loose-legged whore! Our friend, Ah Jun, is the wife! Who is this bitch come with her smelly cunt to dishonor our friend! Our friend is gentle and sweet and doesn't deserve this. We must defend her! If you are her friend, you will follow me!"

All the mah-jong aunties threw down their chips too. Ma had stirred them up into a bunch of hungry hens out for blood. She stirred me up too. I was ready. I had no real attachment to Ah Jun but Ma made me want to go out and lay down my life for her anyway.

Ah Jun, at this point, was weeping even harder. She kept trying to grab Ma's hand and hold her back. She kept worrying that her husband would be angry with her. She kept pleading with Ma to step off. Ma wasn't hearing it. Ma was on a crusade against Low Classy. Nothing would stop her. And I did not want to miss it.

I snuck into the pack, hoping to tag along, but Grandmother noticed and told me not to go. *Stupid Grandmother! I thought. If I can't go to this party, it'll be all her fault.* Grandmother urged Ma not to take me with her and to have me stay with her and Ah Jun instead. But I didn't want to be around Ah Jun and her wailing anymore. I looked at Ma beseechingly, desperately willing her to take me. *Please.*

I should not have doubted. The Squawking Chicken wanted me to see what Low Classy looked like. She wanted me to see what happens to the Low Classy when it's confronted by the righteous. Ma took my hand and stormed out

of the flat, the head of a herd of home wrecker hunters following behind.

We didn't have to go far. Yuen Long wasn't very big back
then and everyone knew everyone else's business, including
where they lived. Pretty soon we'd arrived at Home Wrecker's building. I tried to imagine what she would look like as
we climbed the stairs. I pictured her with big hair and red
lips. She'd be wearing a nightgown under a silk robe, one
side falling off her shoulder. I wondered if we would catch
her doing the sex, whatever that looked like, and I was at
once afraid of seeing it and really excited about seeing it.

Ma rang the bell. An eye appeared at the peephole and
went away. Ma rang the bell again, and again, and again, and
again, and again. Still the Home Wrecker wouldn't answer.
So the Squawking Chicken started squawking: "I know
you're in there. And now I'm telling all your neighbors what
you've done. You want to get in bed with a married man?
You want to call his wife and brag about your slutty ways?
Fine! Then everyone will know what you are—a cheap,
dirty home wrecker!"

Some of the other residents on that floor started opening
their doors to see what was going on. All the other aunties
filled them in on what Home Wrecker had been doing. It
was crazy and amazing and terrifying, I was so overstimu-

lated, I started to cry. Which is when Home Wrecker finally opened the door. There was silence.

Home Wrecker wasn't at all what I expected. Home Wrecker looked exactly like the rabid mah-jong aunties standing behind the Squawking Chicken in front of the Home Wrecker's steel gate. She even looked a little like Ah Jun—she was totally unremarkable. And she seemed really sad. In a small, wavering voice, she implored, "Please leave. Please don't do this here."

The Squawking Chicken had won already. "Do you know me?" Ma asked. Home Wrecker did, but Ma identified herself anyway. "I am Tsiahng Gai [the Squawking Chicken]. Do you know me?"

Again, Home Wrecker nodded.

"I am Ah Jun's friend. You upset my friend, you upset me. You keep your dirty business to yourself, in a hole somewhere, I don't care. But you bring down Ah Jun again and I won't be so kind next time."

And then we left. We headed back down the stairs. When we got to the lobby, Ma turned around and shouted out, "Snacks on me!" When we returned to Grandmother's, she ordered frog congee and fried breadsticks for the whole group. The aunties gave Ah Jun and Grandmother a play-by-play of what went down at Home Wrecker's. When Ah Jun heard that Home Wrecker was intimidated by the Squawking Chicken, she seemed to calm down. Later on, her husband came to pick her up. When he walked in the door, Ma kept playing like he wasn't there, even though he greeted her by name. I remember thinking that Ah Jun's husband was really nice to Ah Jun and how it didn't seem possible that he would ever be mean to her. After they left, Grandmother mentioned that it was nice to see Ah Jun so happy. Ma made a sound with her teeth and said that it would never last with a man like that.

In the taxi on the way home, I asked Ma why she went to all that trouble if she didn't think Ah Jun would be happy in the long run. Ma said that she never wanted me to forget what happens to Low Classy people. She wanted me to see that Low Classy people not only embarrass themselves, they embarrass everyone around them. Ma explained that no matter how well educated I was and how much money I made, if I was Low Classy, no one would ever respect me. She also warned that being Low Classy follows you around for life. Later on that summer, I overheard Ma talking about Home Wrecker during a game at Grandmother's. Home Wrecker ended up moving one town over, to Tuen Mun. Ma's sister lived in Tuen Mun. She couldn't get rid of her home-wrecker reputation there either.

"Daughter, don't ever be Low Classy. You'll never be respected."

∂⑥

Given the Squawking Chicken's lifelong war against the Low Classy, you'd think that she'd be all class, all the time. The fact of the matter is she is a hypocrite. After all, here is a woman who mobilized a battalion against a Low Classy home wrecker from the base camp of a mah-jong den. She wasn't raised in Buckingham Palace. And she doesn't pretend that she was raised there either. Ma has never misrepresented where she grew up. She has never lied about growing up poor, never lied about the fact that she's not educated, never turned her back on her roots. Ma doesn't judge from the top of the mountain. Ma judges from the ground level, which is how she justifies her own behaviors that might be considered Low Classy to others.

Like how she bargains for no tax wherever she is. I've seen her bargain for no tax in a department store, at Chanel and at Costco. It's flea-market rules no matter what. When I call her on this, when I tell her that there's no way they're going to cut her the tax if she pays cash at Pottery Barn, for Christ's sake, her answer is always the same: "It doesn't hurt to ask. That's how you get ahead in life. If you want to be the chump who overspends, go ahead. But I'm not a billionaire leaving you an inheritance. You should learn how to save where you can."

∽◉

For all her hissing at those who are free with their bodies, her peculiar—and arguably Low Classy—body freedoms are displayed without apology. The Squawking Chicken eats with her mouth open. Like everything else she does, it's loud. She chews by smacking her mouth, gnashing the food against her teeth like there's constantly peanut butter stuck to the roof of her mouth, even if it's just rice. I have been pointing this out to her my whole life. And my whole life, her response has been that that's how they eat where she comes from and why am I being so pretentious?

Beyond the eating, there's also the burping and the farting. The Squawking Chicken will burp, straight up, at the table, at home and when we're out, and carry on like nothing happened. It's the same with the flatulence. Jacek is now intimately familiar with Ma passing gas in his company. We'll be at my parents' place and she'll walk by him on the way to the kitchen and let one go. The first time it happened, he thought he was being framed. Was he supposed to admit to something he didn't do? Was he being set up to fail because they didn't want us to be together? Ma noticed that Jacek seemed uncomfortable so she decided to put him at ease: "Sorry," she said. "I am a lot of gas." These are exact words. And it was the last time she apologized for it.

How is farting freely in the presence of others any less Low Classy than pouting? For the Squawking Chicken it comes down to need and intent. Farting, after all, is a natural biological function. Pouting is a contrived motion of the mouth designed to lure and tempt. Pouting portends an ulterior motive. There is nothing concealed about a fart. When you have to go, you have to go. Anywhere. Even in an alley when there's a perfectly serviceable toilet just steps away.

I was visiting Toronto for work and staying over at my friend Gabrielle's instead of staying with my parents. They had sold their large home in Toronto and had moved to an apartment outside the city. Since I work downtown, it was closer for me to stay with Gab instead of commuting an hour from their condo where I don't have a bedroom. They were coming to pick me up from Gab's for dinner. I was watching from the window when they pulled up outside the house. By the time Gab and I made it out the door, Ma was out of the car and Dad was missing.

"Um, where's Dad?" I asked.

"He had to pee."

My father was two doors down, urinating in a lane between houses. It was five o'clock. It was daytime. And my father was pissing on Gab's neighbors' property. When he could have easily just come into Gab's and used her (private, functioning) bathroom.

What's even crazier is that Ma said it like it was totally normal. Like it was completely logical for my dad, who'd just pulled up in a gold Mercedes, by the way, to be taking a leak on a lovely residential street even though he was parked in the driveway of my friend who could have offered him more appropriate facilities.

As you can imagine, I was mortified. Gab was standing next to me having just been told that my father was, at that moment, baptizing an alley a few feet away while my ma just stood there, smiling, as if we'd just had a perfectly ordinary interaction. I tried to change the subject. Ma had just had surgery on her arm to close up the fistula that she'd used when she required regular dialysis. It was a fresh scar running from her elbow to her wrist about an inch wide, red and swollen, hideous. Somehow I thought I could help Gab forget the fact that my father was eliminating in her community—by grabbing my mother's arm and showing her a gaping wound. By this point, Gab was reeling from the Low Classiness of the Luis. Dad chose that moment to reappear.

"Hi Gab, it's nice to see you again." Fresh from relieving himself in an alley, my father offered his hand to Gab, Gab who had a home, with a bathroom, and a sink, in which he could have washed said hand, only he chose to go freestyle instead.

That's so Low Classy.

I couldn't look at Gab. I hurried my parents back into the car. I busted out of there with them like they had just robbed the place. And then, when we were a safe distance away, I wailed.

"WHYYYYYYYYYYYY did you just not go into the house, Dad? Why did you have to pee outside? It's so uncivilized!"

Dad didn't have a chance to respond. It was like I was having an unreasonable tantrum and Ma was just tolerating me. "Daddy had to go. Do you know how long it took us to get here? Traffic was bad. Hold pee for one hour? Daddy can't pee in the Mercedes. This is a nice car."

And that was it. No further explanation required. Ma can always rationalize away her own Low Classy. The wayward youth who leans outside the 7-Eleven is headed for trouble. The Squawking Chicken playing slots at the casino with one leg hitched up on the ledge and a toothpick sticking out of her mouth is simply . . . comfortable.

CHAPTER 10

You Only Need One True Friend

Sometimes the Squawking Chicken's voluntary and stubborn blindness to her own Low Classy ways—the farting, the no-tax haggling—just makes for a quirky, funny story. She is rigid and unwilling to compromise—characteristics that have served her well in difficult times, qualities that form the cornerstone of a formidable spirit, an unwavering, big personality, a personality that has guided me mostly by good example but also, in a very significant way, by showing me how *not* to be.

I don't walk and smoke (anymore). I never jiggle my leg. Pouting feels unnatural and it looks ridiculous. Forget touching, Jacek and I barely acknowledge each other in public. I have adhered to the Squawking Chicken's Low Classy list and often side-eye others for violating it. But where I've broken from her is that objecting to Low Classiness should not prevent you from showing empathy for those who are un-wittingly Low Classy. The same way she sees no contradiction in her moral stance against someone like Low Classy Jane, who, really, is hurting no one with her baby talk and her curious but not necessarily shady friendships with all her paramours, and the Low Classy lack of compassion Ma herself demonstrated toward Jane, who may have just needed some company. It's one thing to observe a standard of comportment—to practice good manners by avoiding Low Classy behaviors like leg jiggling and walking while smoking. But Ma doesn't see the cruelty in criticizing those who've violated those standards. And she certainly doesn't recognize the hypocrisy in the criticism—that while it may be Low Classy to carry on with several men at the same time or home wreck a marriage, it's probably also Low Classy to make a spectacle out of complaining about the two-timer and humiliating the other woman. To say nothing of the effect that humiliation has on other people observing it all go down. I felt bad for Jane when Ma was judging her so openly, just like I was probably feeling bad for the home wrecker when we crashed her apartment. I was only eleven that day and I didn't understand it at the time, why I was sobbing by the time we left, but I realized it was exactly how I felt as a grown-up hearing her attacks on Jane. I was distressed because Ma was bullying them.

This, perhaps, is the Squawking Chicken's greatest flaw: she is severely lacking in empathy. Whatever the reason—be it the code of Low Classy, or the rules of feng shui and fortune-telling, or as a result of her own trials and tribulations—she sucks at a basic principle of human communication: understanding. And because she is so bad at such a crucial element in building relationships, she also sucks at forgiveness and, therefore, friendship.

My roommate in my second and third years of college was a girl named Winnie. Winnie and I met in first year because we were next-door neighbors in the dorm. We weren't close and she wasn't someone I hung out with regularly on weekends when I'd hit up the local student bar scene, but we did play mah-jong together occasionally and when she was selected by the university lottery for one of the coveted double apartments on campus, she asked me if I wanted to live together. I was lazy. I did not want to live off-campus and take the bus in the winter. Living with Winnie, within walking distance to all my classes, even though I didn't know her all that well, was a no-brainer. I said yes.

At the time, my parents were spending most of the year in Beijing. Dad was an executive at a technology training institute and his company approved his proposal to open a branch in China. They left me on my own, then nineteen, to manage my own budget, including rent and living expenses. Winnie's parents also spent most of their time overseas, preferring to stay in Hong Kong through the winter. We were unsupervised and spoiled. From the moment we moved in, Winnie started hosting all-night mah-jong sessions with some of the other residents in the building. I'd join in on the action too and pretty soon, I was cutting class for days at a time either because I was trying to sleep off the mah-jong or because I was still playing mah-jong. All of us smoked heavily at the time. And we rarely cooked. Walking into our apartment was like getting hot-boxed by a combination of tobacco and takeout food. When Winnie wasn't in London playing mah-jong, she'd sneak off to Toronto with her best friend and disappear for days. Initially I tried to do some cleaning in the bathroom and the kitchen when she was gone, but when she returned, the whole place would just turn to shit again with all the people coming in and out for mah-jong. Eventually I just kept my door closed, so my bedroom was the only (reasonably) clean area in what had otherwise become a dump.

In third year I had a boyfriend so I stopped playing so much mah-jong and ended up at his apartment most nights, coming home only once a week or so to change up some clothes. One day I stopped by during one of Winnie's mah-jong sessions. She was sitting at the table holding a fur ball in her lap. I thought it was a rabbit. It ended up being a chinchilla. Winnie seemed like she was super into her chinchilla.

My parents came home to Toronto for spring break that year so I was with them during the week and they drove me back to campus the night before classes resumed. Ma had to use the washroom and wanted to come up. She couldn't cop a squat outside because it was February and freezing. I knew Winnie had been away for spring break too, and since I'd tidied up, sort of, before I left, I figured it wouldn't be so bad. The smell hit us as soon as I opened the door. It was vile. Which wasn't even the worst part. The worst part was that the Squawking Chicken was all over it. She was possessed. She started throwing open cupboards, she lifted all the cushions off the couch, she tore the sheets off my bed, she shook out every piece of clothing in the closet—and there was nothing, nothing to explain the horrifying odor. Except for whatever was behind Winnie's door. I told Ma she couldn't go in there, that it was totally offside.

"This is danger!" she shouted dramatically, as her hand wrapped around the doorknob, her red nails turning upward as she opened the door . . .

It was a fucking mess. There were shavings all over the floor. And little pellets of chinchilla excrement. And a weird milky green substance. Rank. The poor chinchilla lay motionless in its cage. Winnie had forgotten to take it with her. Ma lost her shit.

I kept pleading with her that I'd take care of it. That Winnie would be home soon and that it would be all sorted out. She wouldn't have it. She was threatening to call Winnie's parents. But I couldn't sell out Winnie. I wasn't even sure Winnie had gone home for break and I knew if Ma was able to get hold of Winnie's parents, there was a chance I'd blow her cover. So I bargained. I promised I'd move out of the apartment and not live with Winnie anymore after final semester if Ma would just leave.

The Squawking Chicken always knows when she's getting a good deal. She agreed to go on the condition that I keep my word to find somewhere else to live in fourth year and that I call her as soon as Winnie came back to deal with her dead pet situation. Then she told me I had bad taste in friends. That I had always had bad taste in friends. That my friends always took advantage of me. And that I would jeopardize my life if I kept being friends with people who let their chinchillas rot away in their bedrooms. She proceeded to list off the names of all my friends from middle school through high school and college, calling them all losers. Some of them were, indeed, losers. But not all of them were losers. Some of them were really great people.

"Ma, not all of my friends suck. And I like having friends. I need friends. Everyone needs friends," I argued.

"You only need one true friend."

When I'd come home from school after arguing with my best friend in high school, which is pretty much what best friends in high school do all the time, Ma would say, "You only need one true friend." If a friend was late to meet me, or I was frustrated with a friend over something harmless, like not calling me back when she told me she would, Ma would decide that the friend was worthless, declaring, "You only need one true friend."

Ma wrote off friends quickly. She wrote off Winnie right away because she was so grossed out by the chinchilla death. For me, though, the dead chinchilla was certainly grounds for a fight, but not a breakup. Winnie and I had a lot of fun together. She was spontaneous and carefree, and I enjoyed her company. In the Squawking Chicken's mind? A permanent split was the only option. Just like she cut off Jane, her roommate in the hospital, for flirting with three men on different days, judging her character on the basis of her behavior with her visitors, Ma determined that Winnie was

Low Classy, morally and hygienically. And she was convinced that any continued association with Winnie would result in me becoming morally and hygienically Low Classy.

When Winnie came home that night, I stayed in my room. I heard her next door moving things around and talking on the phone. She was crying. The next day she told me what happened. She was despondent. She knew she'd fucked up. I felt terrible for her. But, still, after a few days passed, I told her that I was moving out. I tried to not make it about the dead chinchilla but I knew she knew. She was all business about it afterward, asking me to take care of my rent and my phone payments and before long, it was the end of April and I was packing up my things. I never saw Winnie again.

It wasn't the first time the Squawking Chicken had sabotaged one of my friendships.

Ma hated my best friend in high school. Georgia was gorgeous and popular and fun, with a bomb-ass body, all curves, and enormous breasts that, as you can imagine, made her one of the favorites among all the boys. We were so close, in that special way girls are close when they're sixteen—we told each other everything, we practically spoke our own language, we loved each other so proudly it made us feel invincible. But the relationship wasn't without drama.

We were the platonic version of a passionate, all-consuming love affair that couldn't last. Looking back, on some level, I was jealous of Georgia. She was the sun. And I was just one of the people lucky enough to be warmed in her presence. With over two decades of distance now from the situation, I realize that that resentment was one of the reasons our connection gradually deteriorated. That's not to say Georgia didn't do her part, but my response to her faults didn't help. Neither did the Squawking Chicken.

Georgia was flighty. She was distracted a lot of the time. It was never intentional, just part of her personality. She had problems focusing. Over time, because of my feelings of inadequacy about being friends with the golden girl, I started to take it personally. But I never shared these feelings with my ma. Because Ma was not supportive of me hanging out with Georgia from the beginning, I tried not to talk about Georgia with her, especially when Georgia and I were in the "honeymoon phase" of our friendship. That didn't stop Ma, however, from sharing with me her opinions of Georgia—all negative. She didn't trust Georgia. She predicted that Georgia would betray me. She thought Georgia was just using me. She warned me that Georgia would bring me down.

Georgia and I did cut class a lot. She wasn't interested in school. She wanted to be an actress and she probably wasn't suited to a conventional learning environment. I was always a good student, but with Georgia, I lost motivation; I just didn't want to miss out on any moments with her. So I ended up failing a couple of classes and having to go to summer school to make up for it. Ma was livid. Believe me, she shamed me for a long time, and publicly, for it. But she also blamed Georgia for how irresponsible I'd become. Realizing that I'd started to ignore her standard criticisms of Georgia, she decided to take a different tactic. Ma used Low Classiness against two-timing Jane from the hospital, but against Georgia her method was Feng Shui Blackmail.

She started telling me that Georgia was bad luck. She pointed out that since Georgia became a fixture in my life, my life was going to shit. She suggested that Georgia had found a home for her own black energy, transferring it to me, while stealing my light. I didn't pay attention to Ma's cautions when Georgia and I were getting along. But as soon as the first hairline fracture appeared in the foundation of our friendship—over something absurdly innocuous, like who was wearing what to the semiformal—Ma's words lodged themselves into that tiny, minuscule gap, resolutely refusing to move until the fissure became an actual break. Every time Georgia and I argued, Ma's words became louder: Georgia was selfish, Georgia was setting me up, Georgia was happy when I wasn't.

By the time I graduated high school and left for college, Georgia and I were starting to drift apart. On the surface we tried to pretend like we'd be friends forever, but on top of all the problems between us that we were ignoring, I was also heading off to new experiences in a different city while she was staying back in Toronto. At first we talked every day; she even came to campus to visit one weekend. But then she told my boyfriend in Toronto that I was flirting with other guys at school—totally true. But still. That's a total girl-code violation. More importantly, though, the Squawking Chicken had called it. Georgia betrayed me. It was over.

Ma considers what happened with Georgia an outright victory, confirmation once again that she is all-knowing and all-seeing. I look back at the situation, however, and wonder what would have happened if Ma had encouraged me to better communicate my feelings to Georgia and talk out our differences instead of letting my resentments and assumptions about her—planted there by Ma in the first place— dictate my approach to our friendship until it became unsalvageable. Ma would say it wasn't worth saving anyway so why waste your time? Sure. But that only holds up if I could honestly admit that I had no accountability for why Georgia and I fell apart. Of course as my mother, Ma was taking my side. But it's not like Ma had any illusions about my lack of perfection in other areas. She was fully capable of pointing out that I wasn't pretty enough to be a beauty queen and she quite happily shamed me when I misbehaved, always in service of teaching a life lesson. And they have almost always been lessons that have served me well over time.

Ma's life lesson about friendship though—"You only need one true friend"—is the only one that I have doubted. And as I've gotten older, I've become more and more resistant to Ma's attempts at sabotaging my friendships. Using Low Classy against a friend, like she did with Winnie, doesn't work on me anymore. Using Feng Shui Blackmail to distance me from a friend doesn't work either.

I have a very good friend named Margot. She was born in the year of the Goat. I was born in the year of the Ox. The Goat is the opposing sign of the Ox. In other words, Goats and Oxen are supposed to be incompatible. Margot and I are indeed very different. She is a contrarian. She will take the other side, just because. She will challenge at every turn. But because of this she makes me better. The Squawking Chicken likes Margot. She doesn't hate Margot like she hated Georgia. She appreciates that Margot has been generous and kind. Margot visited Ma in the hospital and brought her food. There is nothing about Margot's character that Ma can criticize.

Except she's a Goat.

Ma had no issues with my friendship with Margot the

Goat until we started developing a business project together. It was one thing to hang out but it was entirely another to take that to a professional level because, of course, business means money. And the Squawking Chicken is consumed by worrying about money. She's obsessed with her own money and she's equally obsessed about my money. She regularly demands that I tell her how much I have in my savings account. Everything about my career relates back to money. Because Ma is now at an age when money is only spent and not earned, her attitude about money is precious and paranoid. She is terrified about my not having any by the time I retire. And she is anxious about anything or anyone who would take it away. Like a Goat called Margot. Not that she believed Margot had any nefarious intentions, but she worried that Margot's Goat-ness would clash with my Ox-ness; she thought that Margot's longer, sharper goat horns would dominate my shorter, blunter ox horns and that somehow that would result in me going bankrupt.

What Ma didn't understand was that financial gain wasn't the reason Margot and I wanted to collaborate. In fact, it wasn't even a consideration. For us, it was about creativity and fun. What could be more inspiring than imagining a new world with one of your best friends? These are the dreams that begin at sleepovers in grade school, whispered under the covers with the lights turned out, giggling until a parent comes in to tell you to be quiet. These are the experiences the Squawking Chicken never had—both because she's an immigrant and also because she was deprived of that kind of childhood.

It's a common joke I share with all my friends from immigrant families—our parents just didn't get it. Sleep *over*? Sleep away from home? Why would you want to sleep away from home? Some immigrant parents related it to safety: Who are these people? What if they don't give you back? Others related it to diet: What will you eat there? What kind of food do those people serve? The Squawking Chicken, naturally, related it to money: I bought you a bed, such a nice bed. You don't want to sleep in your own bed, you'd rather share a bed with a stranger when there's one you can have to yourself in your own house?

Needless to say, sleepovers weren't happening in Yuen Long, Hong Kong, when Ma was growing up. And even if they were, during the years when she would have had sleepovers, she wouldn't have had the opportunity, having quit school early to care for her siblings and work off her parents' gambling debts. So it's not just that the Squawking Chicken can't appreciate the bonding that can result from a sleepover, she actually missed out on enjoying the small moments that form the building blocks of friendship during those awkward, angsty adolescent years. Through the joys and the mistakes of those moments, we learn how to listen, what happens when we don't listen, how to share, when to hold back, how to comfort, how to hurt—how to Be a Friend.

My ma, the Squawking Chicken, for all her wisdom, doesn't know how to be a friend. I only fully realized this after she was hospitalized for POEMS. One of the women she had met at her Chinese opera lessons, Kimberly, was the opera master's wife. She's very kind, very sweet, so sweet she doesn't even like to gossip, unlike so many of the other ladies who are part of the Chinese opera circle. It's the Chinese version of *The Real Housewives*, except that instead of gossiping while tanning, working out and shopping, they gossip while singing Chinese opera, playing mah-jong and shopping. Kimberly, however, mostly stayed out of the drama. She and Ma quickly became close. Kimberly was one of the few people outside family who came to visit Ma in the hospital when she was at her worst. She went out of her way to help, bringing fresh noodles for Ma on her lunch hour from work because she knew that Ma was having a hard time with the hospital food. She'd skip her own meal just to rush over because she wanted the broth to still be hot by the time she arrived. She never expected anything in return. Ma kept saying how wonderful Kimberly was. She made me promise to take Kimberly and her family out for dinner to thank her for her generosity. I did. But when it was Ma's turn to come through in Kimberly's time of need, she couldn't deliver.

There was a tragedy in Kimberly's family. She lost someone very close to her while she was on a trip back to Hong Kong. Ma had asked Kimberly before she left, well before the sad news, to bring back some Chinese herbs. Kimberly was understandably despondent when she came back to Canada. She stayed in her bedroom while the Chinese opera lessons were happening in the basement. She refused to see anyone, she refused to go out, she was too depressed to socialize. Ma missed Kimberly and wanted to talk to her. So she picked up the phone and called. Kimberly's son, Sean, answered and said that she wasn't feeling up to it. Ever sensitive, the Squawking Chicken told Sean to pass on to his mother that she was phoning about her Chinese herbs.

!!!

I asked Ma about Kimberly a few days after that conversation. She told me what had happened, which is when I explained to her that that was really rude and that if she really wanted to let Kimberly know that she cared, she needed to call back and, this time, not inquire about her fucking herbs and that even if Sean picked up, she should tell him to pass on the message to Kimberly that she was thinking of her and was concerned about her and to call her if she wanted to talk. I also advised her to call every few days, not just once, and keep passing on that message.

It was like I was teaching her how to walk. She had no idea. All her "friend" feelings were there, but she didn't know how to show them, and even when I coached her through the process, she felt uncomfortable expressing them. Ma was sympathetic. But she didn't know how to offer sympathy. She didn't understand that sympathy looks different depending on who it's intended for. She wasn't capable of tailoring her sympathy to the person who's receiving it. She thought it was enough that she was sympathetic in the first place, that her initial phone call would have been enough for Kimberly to make the connection that she was on her mind.

The Squawking Chicken is great in a crisis. She'll come through when the triads are threatening you for money. She'll speak up for you if you need protecting. She'll defend your honor when your husband is cheating on you. She'll have your back when you're being swindled. She is there for the urgent and extraordinary. But she totally sucks for everything in between—those moments between crises that hold friendship together, the moments that make memories.

Memories like working with one of your closest friends on a project. Which is why she couldn't accept that Margot and I wanted to work together. Margot and I were essentially trying to create an adult sleepover. The motivation wasn't money. Being together was the only motivation we needed. Doing it together was what was most exciting. Since Ma has never lived through the thrill of sharing something like that with a friend, she couldn't comprehend why that would be the end goal. In the absence of that understanding, rather than the wonderful personal fulfillment that occurs when two friends find their connection, all she could see was financial risk. This is why the Squawking Chicken fails at friendship. Because her approach to friendship is fundamentally flawed: it's self-preservation at the expense of trust. The Squawking Chicken does not trust. And friendships can't last if there's a constant expectation of betrayal from one side. So Ma has convinced herself that you only need "one true friend."

Ma only keeps in touch with one friend from her childhood. It's my godmother, Auntie Lai, who lives in Hong Kong. They've known each other for over forty years. They used to see each other once every other year, but Ma can't travel long distance anymore due to illness. They speak on the phone every few weeks. Auntie Lai looks after Ma's accounts in Hong Kong. Ma trusts her with her money because Auntie Lai has seen the Squawking Chicken through it all—she knows about her family's disappointments, she watched Ma reclaim her life and pride in young adulthood, she knows why Ma left Dad, she accepted Ma's relationship with Uncle—and she has (ahem) never judged. Auntie Lai didn't judge Ma because she was there when it all happened, their history was shared, she knew the rationale behind Ma's decisions, she knew the heartbreak behind Ma's choices. And yet, even having been on the receiving end of beautiful acceptance and understanding, experiencing the wonderful gift from that "one true friend," Ma is incapable of extending to anyone else the same acceptance and understanding Auntie Lai gave her. Because in her mind, Auntie Lai is the exception, a rare anomaly that only proves her point that you only need one true friend. Like a scientist who refuses any alternative interpretation of data but for the hypothesis she desperately wants to put forward, Ma has willfully chosen to believe that Auntie Lai's version of friendship is not the universal definition of it but a unique and singular representation, a comet never to return again, a once-in-a-lifetime event that cannot be replicated. Any potential new friend then comes in at a disadvantage. They are expected to be a letdown. And they often are, both because no one is infallible but also because Ma goes looking for their flaws. The result, I've noticed, is a maximum friendship life span of eighteen months to two years. At the end of that time, always a breakup.

There was Mrs. Pong in 1999. Ma and Mrs. Pong were

introduced at mah-jong. They clicked quickly and soon it was Mrs. Pong this, Mrs. Pong that. Ma was over at Mrs. Pong's at least three times a week. Ma had me research where Mrs. Pong's kids could go for English language improvement classes because they were new to Canada. Mrs. Pong hooked Ma up when she wanted to buy fake Louis Vuitton handbags. Then Mrs. Pong claimed she found a great abalone supplier and sent over a few pounds for Ma to try. Abalone is a big-ass deal in Chinese homes for its perceived healing properties and because of its cost. Ma is always saying that abalone will boost energy and stimulate the mind. So abalone becomes a double-brag for anyone who has access to it—because they can afford it and also in being able to afford it, they might be smarter than everyone else.

Ma tried Mrs. Pong's abalone and it was terrible. She said the meat was too chewy and that it tasted fake. Since it was such a hot menu item, there was apparently a lot of counterfeit abalone floating around. Rather than giving Mrs. Pong the benefit of the doubt—perhaps she'd been duped by her abalone dealer?—Ma automatically assumed that Mrs. Pong was in on the abalone fraud and using her as an unwitting publicist for her imitation abalone. So she cut her off with no explanation. Mrs. Pong was confused about why she was suddenly shut out of the Squawking Chicken's life. Ma would screen her calls and when other members of their mah-jong circle called to invite her to play at Mrs. Pong's place, she made a big production of telling the caller that she didn't want to say why she couldn't go to Mrs. Pong's because that would be gossipy . . . which, as you can imagine, only made the gossip even worse. When it got back to Mrs. Pong, she went on the offensive, talking shit about Ma to protect herself, and that only confirmed to Ma that she was right all along—Mrs. Pong wasn't a friend worth keeping.

Mrs. Pong was followed by Mrs. Kam in 2003. Mrs. Kam and Ma were friends from their Chinese opera singing club. (Chinese people who emigrate are constantly looking for "activities." These range from salsa dancing to calligraphy to winemaking. Ma came home after one of those winemaking classes with two cases of ice wine that she's still giving away. Every time she sees my friends she comes with her goddamn ice wine that tastes like shit.) Mrs. Kam and the Squawking Chicken were the unofficial social activities coordinators of the group. They organized all kinds of excursions for the other Chinese ladies who were new to the community. They planned a big Chinese New Year feast to raise money for charity. Like she was at the beginning with Mrs. Pong before her, Ma was tight with Mrs. Kam. They had dim sum several times a week. They went to every new Chinese restaurant opening to get the jump on the best place to eat. There was a lot going on with Mrs. Kam all the time. Until Ma started noticing that when Mrs. Kam wasn't with her, she was spending a lot of time with the married calligraphy teacher.

Ma claims that this was brought to her attention by other calligraphy students who saw Mrs. Kam staying late after the sessions. A few weeks later, the calligraphy master presented Mrs. Kam's calligraphy as one of the feature pieces in his galley show, even though, as some sniped, she didn't have the best technique. Well, that was enough for Ma to brand Mrs. Kam a home wrecker. She started distancing herself from Mrs. Kam, again without warning. Mrs. Kam tried to figure out why the Squawking Chicken wouldn't talk to her anymore, but when Ma refused to engage, Mrs. Kam not only gave up, she also managed to convince everyone else to side with her and they did because she carried so much favor with the calligraphy teacher. Ma once again had to go look for a new group of friends, declaring that this group was beneath her.

Mrs. Kam was followed by Mrs. Seto. Mrs. Seto preceded someone else I can't remember. Nowadays, whenever I'm introduced to the flavor-of-the-month friend, I make a bet with myself about how long this one will last. Will it be right on the eighteen-month mark? How close will she get to the two-year mark? But as easy as it was for the Squawking Chicken to walk away from her friends, it's not like it was super hard for them to let her go either. By expecting them to be perfect, she set them up to fail. In not forgiving them when they failed, she protected herself from further disappointment. At the same time, though, without trust, why would anyone want to stick around? And when they inevitably walked away? The Squawking Chicken's explanation for it was because "they're jealous."

Sometimes they were. And sometimes they were just annoyed.

Not only is the Squawking Chicken impatient, judgmental and unforgiving, she's also a chronic boaster. My parents bought a home in a new development in Toronto in 1991. They were in their forties. They had worked hard to be able to afford a big house—four bedrooms, three and a half bathrooms, a big yard, a big basement and an open kitchen. They upgraded all the materials, choosing marble countertops, ceramic tile, hardwood floors and a custom, curved offset staircase that was the centerpiece of the first floor as soon as you walked in the front door. Ma loved her house. She was so proud of the house. She was proud of what it represented—Dad's success and their tenacity. When we first moved in, we had people over all the time. And whenever they'd come over, she'd give them every single detail—with dollar figures. It was the ultimate in braggadocious. The Chinese are a boastful culture to begin with. (See the Beijing 2008 Olympic Games Opening Ceremony.) We are very good at showing off in your face with an explosion. The Squawking Chicken's voice already sounds like an explosion, so when the debris that's blasting in your ears is all about the best this and the best that and how much it costs to be the best, well, I'm her daughter and I can understand why someone would become a hater.

There were about fifty people invited to my parents' housewarming party. I was eighteen at the time, acutely sensitive to what other people thought and therefore very sensitive to Ma's over-the-top behavior. Ma didn't wait long before ushering people through the house, touring them through all the highlights. When she came to the staircase, she walked almost all the way up to the top while her audience stood at the bottom, and then slowly and theatrically made her way down, her red nails trailing along the bannister, explaining in Cantonese: "This staircase was custom designed. No one else on the block has a staircase like ours. The wood was imported from Italy. It took them an additional two weeks to construct it beyond the deadline. But we understood, because we paid them fifty thousand dollars extra to make it happen."

I could swear I saw half the people there rolling their eyes. I mean it was a nice staircase but it wasn't a scene from a movie, you know? Later on, when everyone left, I told Ma that she shouldn't be so boastful, that it might turn people off if she talked about money that way. Her response: "Why you so embarrassing your dad? Your daddy work hard. Your daddy buy a big house. Be proud of your daddy!"

I've learned to live with the Squawking Chicken's boasting. As my career has progressed, I've also become a reluctant accomplice in it. My phone will ring. Ma's on the other end, overly enthusiastic. That's the first sign she's not alone. "Hi Elaine! I watched you on the TV just like you asked me to!" (I did not ask her to.) "I'm here with all the aunties playing mah-jong. What a pretty dress you wore today! But tell the makeup artist not to go so heavy on your eyebrows next time, okay? Bye!" So she is at mah-jong. And she made a point of stopping the game to turn on the television, just in time to see me reporting on television. The excuse was that I asked her to. The truth is that she wanted to show off the fact that her daughter is on national television to all her friends.

If my picture is in a magazine or a newspaper, she'll buy enough copies to pass around at dim sum. If I'm heading to L.A. for the Oscars, she'll somehow work the conversation around to that. If Mrs. Jiang's daughter is getting married in France, Ma will let everyone know that I'm covering the royal wedding in England. The Squawking Chicken is a classic conversation hijacker.

Her rationale for the boasting and the showing is always

the same: people shouldn't be so insecure, just like I shouldn't have been "so embarrassing" about my daddy. As long as the intent behind her words is not to hurt or to put down, she sees nothing wrong with being overtly proud of her daughter and her husband's accomplishments. If they were her "true friends," they'd be happy for her instead of being resentful. The fact that they choose to be insulted by her boasting is more a reflection on their lack of confidence and not her lack of tact. And to be fair, Ma is genuinely happy for people when they boast back. It doesn't offend her. She has the self-assurance to not draw comparisons and be jealous. So I don't totally disagree with her assessment about people's insecurities. But the problem is that those who are put off by the Squawking Chicken's boasting haven't been given any background to soften the blow of it. They don't know where she came from. They don't know about her difficult childhood, her irresponsible parents, the way she had to fight for everything she's achieved. She hasn't trusted them to share that information. Without the courtesy of disclosure, of sharing, all they have is the boasting at face value. In the gap between disclosure and boasting grows disdain.

I can appreciate the Squawking Chicken's need to boast. I know where it comes from. But I can also understand why her friends, now ex-friends, would be put off by it, because they don't know.

And so Ma's revolving door of friends has only further cemented her belief in her motto: "You only need one true friend." The more friends she breaks up with, the more wary she becomes of mine. When I try to tell her that my friends aren't like that, she always brings it back to Sally.

Sally and the Squawking Chicken went to school together in Yuen Long. The Squawking Chicken dropped out for family obligations. Sally was sent to study overseas. They kept in touch through letters and phone calls. Sally was already installed in Canada when Ma immigrated with Dad. Sally helped Ma find a job as a waitress. Ma thought she and Sally were blood sisters. Ma agreed to be godmother to Sally's son. Sally and her husband, Don, scrounged and saved for years to open their own restaurant and in 1989, they leased a property in a small town about an hour outside Toronto. They asked Dad to go into business with them. (We were on holiday with Sally and Don when my parents decided to have sex in the same room as me and ruin my life.) Sally and Don looked after the kitchen and the staff. Dad managed the accounts. We all had to pitch in. I spent weekends there bussing tables and packing takeout orders. Whenever Ma came to visit from Hong Kong—to renew her Canadian passport, attend a wedding—she would get to work as the hostess and put on an apron if it got really busy. Together, Sally, Don and my parents ran a thriving small business. The restaurant was a community favorite. Though it closed down in 2008 after nineteen years, people in the neighborhood still remember the quality and variety of the food. We weren't just serving chicken balls and egg rolls, we also mixed it up with some traditional, delicious Chinese dishes. But it couldn't last forever.

Don went back to Hong Kong in 2000 for several weeks, leaving Sally solely in charge of the restaurant. Returning home was a sort of pilgrimage. When he left China, he had been a poor farm boy, kind of awkward, and no one really expected much of him. When he returned, he was a successful entrepreneur. Don wanted people to see what he had made of himself. Don wanted people to know he didn't end up a loser. But even though Don had changed his circumstances, he still felt like the gangly kid who was made fun of at school. At some point during his trip, Don met a woman who flattered him with compliments—about his business, about his wealth, about his intelligence. I'll say this about Don—no one worked harder, but he wasn't blowing anyone away with his smarts. Don is the guy, though, who needs to believe that he's the brains behind the operation. As his wife, Sally let him believe the glory, even though she was the one who held it all together, always cleaning up his messes. Now along came a woman who knew exactly what to say to him. Don was done. He fell in love. He wanted to leave Sally.

Sally begged him to reconsider. She promised she would forgive him. She just wanted him to come home. The problem for Don, however, was that the business was half in Sally's name. Ma urged Sally to use this as a negotiating card and to never give up her half of the restaurant. When Don came home, Ma told Dad to watch the accounts, to make sure Don wasn't taking money from the business to keep his other woman happy. Don carried on with his mistress for over a year, all while trying to convince Sally to sell, so that he could take his share and start his new life with his new woman. Sally didn't want to sell. The restaurant was her soul. She didn't know what she would do with herself if she wasn't working. So she compromised. She told Don that he could go back to Hong Kong and see his lover as much as he wanted. And when he was in Canada, he could call her long distance and keep up the relationship, so long as they could still share a home, still share a life. Who wouldn't take that deal?

After Sally worked out the arrangement with Don, she stopped communicating with the Squawking Chicken. Maybe she didn't want to face Ma's disapproval while feeling the shame of her own compromise. Or maybe she was much happier this way and had no time for Ma's judgment. Whatever the real reason, Ma never found out the answer. Because after forty years of friendship, Sally just dropped out. And right when Ma needed her most.

Ma's kidneys had shut down a few years before and she was awaiting a transplant. In 2002 she finally got the call. Sally didn't make contact. Ma's transplant came and went, Sally didn't visit, she didn't call. Ma felt completely abandoned by her friend, someone she'd known most of her life. From then onward, Dad continued to look after the books, to make sure the finances were legit, but Ma never went to the restaurant again. And when the opportunity came up in 2008 to finally sell their share of the business, Dad got out of it quickly. We don't know what happened to Sally and Don, whether or not they're still together, what they decided to do next. And where the restaurant used to be, there's now a Taco Bell. That could very well be a metaphor for Ma's attitude about friendship: fast food, fast friends.

The Squawking Chicken's disenchantment with her own friends has colored the way she sees me interacting with mine. She is constantly paranoid that the same will happen to me. She counsels caution over caring, protection over sharing. She'll use everything at her disposal to manipulate me into choosing Me over my Friends.

Ma's been betrayed and disappointed so much in her life, by so many different kinds of friends. In her experience, friendship has only resulted in bitterness and inconvenience, a lot of wasted emotion. Therefore, friendship in the Squawking Chicken's mind is not worth the self-sacrifice.

My own experience with friendship has been profoundly the opposite. I have more than "one true friend." In fact, I have many great friends. They are wonderful, interesting people who bring wisdom and color into my life. They are accepting and forgiving of me. I am grateful and faithful to them. And I keep trying. Every day I try to be a good friend. I learned how to be good at friendship from the Squawking Chicken. Inadvertently, in being such a shitty friend, she taught me how to be a better one. She showed me the overwhelming loneliness that can result from refusing to share, from the fear of being open, from being too afraid to trust. So I chose instead to believe in the power of friendship. To believe that for every friend who fails you, there will be one who won't. And before long, you look around, and suddenly the ones who are still standing become your soldiers for life. Sometimes I think that it's one of the best gifts the Squawking Chicken has ever given me, albeit accidentally. She may not have intended it to turn out this way, but her inability to forge lasting friendships ended up helping me forge some of the most meaningful relationships I'll ever have. And I often wonder whether or not it was part of a larger purpose. Every hurt and regret Ma has ever accumulated ended up as a plus in my column. For every time she was ever put down, I would rise later. Every time she started over was every advantage I've ever had. Every friend who ever left meant more friends for me.

A part of me believes that Ma took her losses so that I could have my wins. That for all the times the odds were so heavily stacked against her, she accepted them so that in turn, hopefully, they'd be stacked in my favor. Ma's always told me that good fortune comes in waves—there is a crest and there is a fall. Like in life, without darkness there would be no light. But what if she was the one eating all the falls, swallowing all the dips, welcoming all the darkness, so that I could ride one long wave all the way to shore? What if that's the deal she made with the gods of feng shui and fortune-telling? That she would sacrifice herself so that I could soar instead?

During the lowest point of her illness while she was hospitalized for nine months, when Dad would go home at the end of visiting hours, Ma would call me because she was too uncomfortable to sleep. By this time, she had lost a quarter of her body weight. There was no fat on her body to cushion the sharpness of her bones. I knew she was in pain. And I knew that she had to endure it all by herself for hours in that hospital bed, surrounded by strangers, until Dad came back the next afternoon. I lived in Vancouver then, which is three hours behind Toronto, so we talked for hours, until the exhaustion set in. She wanted to know about my day, about my business; even though she barely understood the information I was giving, she still wanted to hear that Jacek and I were working hard and making plans. These plans excited her. They motivated her to get better because she wanted to be able to enjoy seeing us achieve our goals. Our conversations ended up being repetitive. Day after day, I was giving her the same information. But she had no one else to talk to. Ours were the only lives she could share in.

One night, the sadness of her situation was too much. I wept into the phone. She asked me why I was crying and I told her that I felt sorry for her—that she was so sick, that she was so alone, that she had no friends.

"You only need one true friend," she said. "*You* are my one true friend."

I am the Squawking Chicken's only daughter and her only true friend. It can be a burden, sure. But, mostly, it is my life's honor.

Epilogue

There is no cure for POEMS. Ma has regained the weight but the symptoms come and go. She's able to move her legs now but she will never be able to walk again without leg braces. So she and Dad have made several lifestyle adjustments to accommodate her disability. Everything just takes longer now. And they don't go out as much. We installed a kick-ass satellite system in her apartment so she can watch all the Chinese TV she wants. And the Squawking Chicken has recently learned how to text. It has added a new dimension to our communication, making *boe doe*-ing a lot easier, and more annoying. She frequently texts me after she watches me on television to provide feedback—often about my face. She also uses texts to force her way into my house. Ma's specialty is Chinese medicinal soup. Which she harasses me about constantly via text. Every soup has a purpose. One kind of soup is "good for the lung." Another is "good for the skin." There's a soup for every body part. And the soup delivery schedule is frequently decided over text message, along with a few other random insights.

The Squawking Chicken texts exclusively in ALL CAPS. Here are some of her messages:

Sep 19/1:09PM

WHERE R U

Sep 19/1:12PM

I BRING SOUP

Sep 19/1:15PM

YOUR BAD SKIN NEED SOUP

Sep 19/8:34PM

DID U DRINK SOUP

Sep 19/8:50PM

DRINK SOUP TONIGHT IF U FINISH I MAKE
GINSING SOUP TOMORROW GOOD FOR LIVER LET
ME KNOW

Listen to the Squawking Chicken

Sep 20/2:20PM

NICE SHOW GOOD SKIN EVERY ONE LOOK

PRETTY AND SKINY

Sep 24/2:06PM

STOP MAKE UGLY FACE WHEN YOU TALKS

Sep 25/2:11PM

NO MORE UGLY FACE BETTER

Oct 8/9:22PM

WHY JACEK NO DRINK SOUP

Oct 8/9:28PM

JACEK DRINK SOUP

Oct 8/10:30PM

DRINK SOUP FOR JACEK GOOD FOR SPLEEN

Oct 15/10:31AM

EAT PAPAYA SO YOU NO FAT

Oct 28/2:20PM

U LOOKS SKINNY HA HA HA R U WANT ORANGE

[No idea what this means]

Oct 29/2:45PM

YOU LOOKS NICE TODAY AND TALKING GOOD

Oct 29/2:49PM

GOOD SHOW GOOD GIRL

Acknowledgments

To Deirdre Molina, because you waited six years, and then had to hold my hand for eight months. Thanks for the nights at the Beacher Café, and for enjoying my meat loaf.

To the wise and brilliant Amy Einhorn for all the exclamation points—they didn't come easy so when I got them from you, I knew it was all going to be okay. I will never delete that email. There's a little Squawking Chicken in you too!

To Amy Moore-Benson, because without you, none of it would be possible. That we came back together after all that time is one of my favorite stories.

To Gab—for the seemingly interminable torture sessions and your work (pro bono) and all the dinners and especially for letting my dad pee on your street. I'm not really sorry about that and I don't think you'd want me to be either.

To Fiona—it started that weekend in Portland, so let's start planning more trips, more breakfasts, more us. Thank you for being my best friend.

Acknowledgments

To Duana—because you understood, having been there before, when I hated everything, and you were never worried. So when will it be your turn?

To Nanci—for bringing me here, and making almost every day like cupcakes. You fight for and support your people. It's a privilege to be one of them.

To Crespi—for Paris, London, New York and L.A. And everything that happened in between.

To our "child" Emily—for the long days and looking after home base. Thank you for being loyal, trustworthy and so dedicated.

To Dex—for that great day at my house when you got her to smile.

To Lucky—for that great day at my house when she let you do her makeup, and approved!

To Jordan Schwartz—for giving me that first chance. I will remember it forever.

To Morley Nirenberg and the *etalk* family—for every exclusive experience, for Oscars and Junos and TIFFs, but mostly for letting me be part of a winning team.

To everyone at *The Social*—for having my back, letting me sing through the office, rant about my poo, and for putting up with "Complainey." Now please pass the microphone.

To Michelle Clausius and Covenant House Vancouver—for embracing me before it all began, for encouraging me when it started and for sending me off but always welcoming me back.

To everyone at CTV Communications, Random House of Canada and Penguin—for rallying, cheering and protecting when necessary.

Acknowledgments

To Darren Roberts—for listening to me bitch about that first chapter, and telling me to get to work.

To Oliver, Noah and Veronica—because you're the only ones I'll get to squawk at. Are you ready?

For Ewa and Stan—for loving your Chinese daughter.

For Dad—for driving me everywhere, for picking me up at whatever time of night, for not saying much, but you never had to. I always knew.

For Jacek, the most patient, the most generous, the most kind, and the most long-winded. Thank you for putting up with my shit. Every word in the "Paris" card, and so much more.

And for the readers of LaineyGossip.com—it would never have happened without your visits, without your emails, without you coming back. Thank you, love you, owe you. I will always be Yours in gossip, Lainey.